The Resourceful Cook

The Resourceful Cook

or

What to Cook When There's Nothing to Cook

Elizabeth Ray

BOOK CLUB ASSOCIATES
LONDON

This edition published 1978 by
BOOK CLUB ASSOCIATES
by arrangement with
MACMILLAN LONDON LIMITED

Printed in Great Britain by
THE ANCHOR PRESS LTD
Tiptree, Essex

Bound in Great Britain by
WM BRENDON & SON LTD
Tiptree, Essex

Contents

How to use this book

IN THE DAYS when a household had a Cook, with other staff to help her so that she just *cooked* (I suppose there may be some still), one recognition of her importance was that she was known as Mrs, regardless of her actual marital status (a point that no one now would worry about, and indeed might actually object to). Madam would discuss the day's menus with Cook, telling her what was required for which meal, and for how many. The butcher, the baker, the grocer and everyone else would call round for orders which would be delivered forthwith, and the gardener or green-grocer would produce the vegetables. She worked hard, as families were bigger and entertained more formally – indeed, if the house-hold were big enough she had to organise two, or even three kinds of meals – one for upstairs, one for downstairs and one for the nursery. She was also treated with respect and a certain amount of awe, and as she had probably started her career as kitchenmaid and worked her way up, she knew it all. But above all, what she was required to do was one thing – to cook.

Now, the great majority of housewives – or at any rate those who are interested in this kind of book – fit in the cooking with all the other household chores, families and maybe a job. Deliveries are either occasional (in the country) or non-existent (in most towns). Early closing is always on the day she has to wait in all morning for the man who says he is coming to mend the television first thing and arrives at four o'clock. The slog round the super-market makes for mental indigestion, while many a carefully planned meal has to be abandoned because the crucial ingredient happens not to be available in the shop that day, so she has to hunt desperately for a substitute. Finally the friends who 'dropped in for a drink' stay on and on, so that unless they are all going to fall flat on their faces with hunger and alcohol, they have to be fed, or the children come home accompanied by assorted friends saying, 'I told them it would be all right and you wouldn't mind'.

But for the woman who plans her shopping and storage carefully there are advantages which great-grandmother's Cook did not have. She has a far greater variety of food available, wherever she lives. She has a refrigerator and possibly a freezer to supplement her store-cupboard; and in one monthly visit she can load the car at the supermarket with all her basic ingredients.

This book tries to give ideas of how to make the most of the foods that anyone can have in the house at any one time. It is not a book to be followed slavishly day by day, meal by meal, but one which tells you how to turn those basic ingredients into a meal on those days when shopping is difficult, the purse empty, ideas are non-existent, or the delicious dinner for two has to be extended into an equally delicious dinner for four.

The main thing for the resourceful cook is to see that there are certain basic ingredients *always* available, and to restock them when they are running low. Most households have room for a reasonable store-cupboard, and many of the essential ingredients keep well. They need not all be bought at once, nor are they necessarily used up at one go, so there need not be vast expenditure each week to keep the store-cupboard up to strength.

The longest-lasting basic ingredients, such as tins of anchovies, tuna, corned beef and so on, should keep for at least a year and some for several years; semi-perishables like flour, potatoes, U.H.T. (Long-Life) milk and cream, Parmesan, stock cubes and the like keep for anything from six months to a year, while even the more perishable foods like eggs, butter and bacon will keep for more than a week in a refrigerator. So unless you have no storage space at all or have to hump everything home in your two arms you need only have one major expedition each week, and still know you can withstand a small siege. It is particularly important to keep well stocked in the winter if you live in the country, when getting about is not always easy, so that you can laugh at the weather.

But stock up sensibly. Resist the 'special offer' in the supermarket which sits on the store-cupboard shelf, unused and unusable for years. And remember the story by Roger Longrigg, called 'Sing a Song of Ninepence' and published in *The Compleat Imbiber*

No 10, of a group snowed up in Scotland over Christmas with only the Fortnum's hamper they had had sent to them. After a daily diet of pâté de foie gras, marrons glacés, brandied peaches, caviar and the like, with only Cointreau to drink, tempers got a little frayed (if I remember rightly, two marriages foundered over that Christmas) and they could think only of porridge and tea. You can get tired of fancy food far more quickly than anything else, but 'wholesome' food doesn't have to be dull. Readers of Beatrix Potter's *Two Bad Mice* will recall the fun the mice thought they would have eating up all the delicious looking food in the doll's house, only to find that when they finally got to it 'the fish was glued to the dish', and it was all plaster. One mouse was called Hunca Munca, and I call such food – the kind that looks lovely and tastes of nothing, is all show and no reality – Hunca Munca food. Whatever else I have tried to do in this book, and some may find the fare plain, I have tried very hard not to suggest Hunca Munca food.

Of course, not everyone will consider everything on my basic list is necessary. Keep in store the things that suit you and your family. I have tried to avoid leaning too heavily on tins and not at all on home freezers. Many people don't have them and there is plenty of literature for those who do. Also frozen main meals often take a long time to thaw. Freezers and the ice compartments of ordinary refrigerators are, however, a very useful alternative storage for such basic items as stock, breadcrumbs, pastry, etc.

And now for the lists of what *I* always like to have at hand, to which you can add indefinitely according to your own taste. I have divided them into three sorts: non-perishables – mainly tinned or dried goods which keep well for over a year; the every-day essential perishables (dairy food, vegetables, fruit, etc.) which last only a few weeks and some dry goods which deteriorate within a few months, and the flavourings, seasonings and other 'extra' ingredients, either bought or home-made, which may not make a meal in themselves but are fundamental to its interest. I have expressly excluded fresh meat and fish from the lists, as they are not part of the basic store-cupboard, but there are some recipes in the book which use up left-over fish and meat.

Store-cupboard ingredients

Non-perishables

All these goods should keep in good condition for well over a year. You can augment them by the old-fashioned way of preserving in bottles and jars, to make the most of fruit or vegetables in season. Tomatoes bottle very well, and if you grow your own, or you can buy them cheaply, they are well worth doing, and even the pale, hard, English tomato changes in flavour after bottling, becoming more like the strongly flavoured Italian variety. Blackberries – available at the cost of a few scratches, and the feeling that you are getting something for nothing – also bottle well. Jams, chutneys and so on are really only worth doing if you have your own fruit or can buy it cheaply – though the home-made variety usually tastes nicer than the shop kind.

When practical, I prefer to keep dry ingredients in glass jars rather than packets as it is so much easier to see how much there is. Nothing is more annoying than to see a packet on the shelf only to find that there is but a spoonful left inside. If it is in a jar, it is far less easy to overlook the dwindling stock. Dry goods also deteriorate less in glass jars with properly airtight stoppers.

1. TINS

Anchovies
Consommé
Corned beef
Cream
Frankfurters
Ham
Kipper fillets
Mushrooms (or dried)
Pâté
Petits pois
Pimentoes (or dried)
Salmon
Sardines and/or pilchards
Shrimps or prawns
Tomatoes
Tomato purée
Tuna fish

2. PRESERVES AND DRIED GOODS

Apricots
Beans (haricot and
   butter)
Chocolate (plain)
Coffee (ground and
   instant)
Cornflour
Jam (apricot and
   redcurrant jelly)
Lentils
Matzo meal (medium)
   which can be used
   instead of breadcrumbs

for coating fishcakes,
   rissoles and so on
Mayonnaise (in tubes)
Milk (powdered)
Onions (dried)
Prunes
Raisins
Semolina (for *gnocchi* or
   as a coating instead
   of breadcrumbs)
Sugar (white and
   demerara)
Sultanas

Perishables

Eggs, onions, tomatoes, rice, cheese, milk are the absolutely basic everyday perishable foods and it is heartening to know how much a good soup – and soups are easy and economical to make – or a sauce, or an unusual way of cooking vegetables will bring new life to very plain food. Meals don't have to have fish or meat to make them balanced and satisfying. I recall in a particularly lean period producing various vegetable, cheese and egg dishes, saying brightly 'a *jour maigre* today' and my son saying 'Why can't we have a *jour maigre* every day?' – which made it into a *jour de fête* for me.

Date-stamping of food is becoming much more common now, and this is helpful if buying perishable food. Bacon joints, of the cheaper cuts, are good to have in, as they can be used to give the meaty content to many a dish, whether minced, sliced or cooked whole and then used cold. The same with the smoked boiling sausage, which makes a satisfying hot dish served with whatever vegetables you have by you, or can be sliced as it is and used with salad.

Pancakes can be made and stored in the refrigerator until needed, then served with a savoury or sweet filling. Home-made meat or fish pâtés or potted meats also keep well for several days. If you are not confident of making good pastry, the chilled or frozen kind or the pastry mixes, particularly for flaky pastry, are good standbys, and the uses to which pastry can be put are immense.

Cheese is very versatile in use, and I always try to keep in some Parmesan, as it is strongly flavoured, but also a hard milder cheese like Cheddar, and a cream cheese like Philadelphia which also keeps well and can be used for sweet or savoury dishes. Plain yogurt, which you can make at home if you like, keeps better than cream, acts instead of cream in a lot of dishes, making them less rich, and goes well in savoury sauces too.

Salad stuffs, especially lettuce, keep well in plastic containers, and both bacon and cheese keep better in plastic boxes than in greaseproof paper or even foil. But aluminium foil is essential for wrapping things, lining tins or making lids for dishes that haven't any, for the refrigerator or the oven.

1. DAIRY AND MEAT

Bacon (rashers, or a piece which is often cheaper)
Butter
Cheese (Cheddar, Parmesan, cream)
Cream (U.H.T.)
Cream, sour
Eggs
Lard or dripping
Milk (fresh and U.H.T.)
Sausage (smoked boiling ring)
Yogurt

2. FRUIT AND VEGETABLES

Apples (cooking and dessert)
Carrots
Lemons
Onions
Oranges
Peas (freeze-dried Surprise)
Potatoes
Tomatoes (and any other salad stuff)

3. DRY GOODS

Bread
Flaky pastry mix
Flour (plain; self-raising; 'strong' or wholemeal)
Pasta (macaroni; noodles; spaghetti)
Rice (long grain or all-purpose, unless you are very fond of rice pudding)
Suet

Seasonings, flavourings, etc.
A comprehensive stock of seasonings and flavourings are what
transform your basic stores into a variety of delicious meals.

Herbs can be grown in pots if you have no garden, but although
some dry well, most take on a rather peppery taste with no
distinction; the small pots of dry Provençal mixed herbs last a
long time and keep their flavour well. Bayleaves are useful fresh
or dried and you can always have a decorative bay tree in a tub.
Tarragon is one of the most magical of herbs, I think, and every
year I put several sprigs into a bottle which I top up with wine
vinegar – the sprigs can be left in all year – which means that all
year round you can get the flavour of fresh tarragon in salads, or
in many cooked dishes.

Vinegar makes me think of wine: never throw away the last
drops left in the bottles of wine – they can go towards enriching
stews or gravies, and if kept well-corked stay good for a long
time, and can always be added to. Keep one bottle of white and
one of red on the go. And, although initially expensive, Madeira
is a marvellous standby and even when opened never loses its
character. Wine vinegar is more expensive than malt, but far more
delicate and if you keep adding a little left-over wine to a bottle
of wine vinegar you can keep perpetuating your supply, which is
worth doing to save the cost alone. Wine or wine vinegar are
essential for making marinades, which are very useful for making
meat more tender and flavoury before cooking. The simplest is a
mixture of oil, red wine and herbs, in which the meat is left for a
few hours. A good idea is to put the marinade in a plastic bag
(which you then put into a dish in case it leaks) and then add the
meat, as this way you need less liquid than if it were poured over
the meat in an open dish.

Keep in lots of seasonings so that you can ring the changes on
flavours. Worcestershire sauce is an old favourite, but Angostura
bitters, more usually known as an ingredient in pink gin, is also
useful in the kitchen as a rather subtle flavouring. Mustard can
be used generously in cooking, particularly in sauces, as it loses
a great deal of its 'heat', but leaves behind a piquancy that keeps
many guests wondering what it is. A tablespoon of French
mustard added to cheese sauce is excellent. A teaspoon of made
mustard mixed with the egg yolk when making mayonnaise

seems to reduce the chance of it curdling. French mustard is better for most cooking purposes than English as it is milder, but use a yellow one when the colour matters.

Keep a jar of caster sugar with a vanilla pod in it for flavouring custards and such like. It's much nicer, and cheaper in the end, than buying it specially, for although the pods are expensive they last a very long time.

Some good store-cupboard ingredients can be made at home when you have time. Caramel colouring is good for improving the appearance of pallid soups, stews and sauces without altering the flavour, and is much cheaper than buying gravy browning. The recipe is on page 26. A brown *roux* (recipe **No 2**) can also be made in some quantity when you have time, and can be kept in the refrigerator. This acts as a thickening and enriching agent to a savoury sauce and as all the long work is done when you have time, the actual sauce-making is very quick, which is useful if you are in a hurry. Stock keeps for several days in the refrigerator and is the basis of many good soups.

I keep a screwtop jar of dried savoury breadcrumbs for coating fried foods. Dry crusts or left-over bread gently in the oven, then crush it with a rolling pin. If you put the bread in a plastic or greaseproof paper bag first the crumbs are kept nicely in one place without having to be scooped up afterwards. I crumble in a little dried onion and a pinch of salt to give more flavour. You can use bread sauce mix as a substitute, and fine matzo meal or semolina also make good coatings.

Anchovy essence
Angostura bitters
Arrowroot
Bicarbonate of soda
Breadcrumbs, soft and
    dried (see above)
Capers
Caramel colouring (see
    page 26)
Celery salt
Cider, which can be used
    instead of white wine
Curry powder
Garlic, fresh, minced or
    salt
Gelatine
Gherkins
Herbs, as many as
    possible but
    particularly, mint,
    parsley, tarragon,
    chives, marjoram,
    rosemary, bayleaves,
    and a pot of dried

herbs from Provence
Lemon juice
Liqueurs, miniatures are
useful, especially the
orange ones such as
Grand Marnier or
Cointreau
Madeira
Mustard, English and
French
Olives
Peppercorns, black
Pepper, white
Roux, brown (see
page 18)
Salt
Soy sauce
Spices, as many as
possible but
particularly allspice,
cinnamon, cloves,
coriander, ginger,
mace, nutmeg,
paprika, saffron
Stock cubes, chicken
beef or vegetable
Vanilla sugar (see
page 15)
Vinegar, wine or
flavoured (see
page 14)
Wine, red and white (see
page 14)
Worcestershire sauce
Yeast (dried)

Sauces

ONCE UPON A TIME it was said that we were a nation of seventeen religions and only one sauce. What I have never discovered is what that particular sauce was. Anyway, it is not quite true; we have a few more sauces than that and if you take into consideration the sauces that came from India in the eighteenth and nineteenth centuries, such as Worcestershire, originally from an Indian recipe but manufactured in Worcestershire; ketchup, which is a corruption of an Indian word; and many others that date back to that time alone, it is clear that we have far more than seventeen sauces, let alone religions.

As well as the spicy sauces and ketchups there are the variants of the flour – butter – liquid base, and many others besides. Here is a very small selection of easily made sauces, from easily available ingredients.

1 Basic White Sauce
Time taken: 15–20 mins

1 oz (25 g) butter
1 oz (25 g) flour
1 pint (6 dl) milk
salt and pepper

Melt the butter in a saucepan, add the flour and stir together for a few moments, without letting it colour. Add one pint of hot milk gradually, stirring all the time so that it does not go into lumps but thickens smoothly. Let it come to the boil and simmer for about ten minutes. Add salt and pepper to taste. Use less milk for a thicker sauce, or more if a pouring sauce is required.

2 Brown Sauce

Time taken: 40 mins

1 oz (25 g) butter
1 oz (25 g) flour
1 medium onion, finely
chopped (if liked)

1 pint (6 dl) stock or vegetable
water
salt and pepper

Melt the butter in a saucepan (and the onion, if used, and let it cook gently until the onion is transparent). Add the flour, stir well and cook together very slowly until the flour is a warm brown colour, which will take about fifteen minutes. This is the brown *roux*. Add the hot meat stock or vegetable water, stirring well until it thickens smoothly, season with salt and pepper and let the sauce simmer for about half an hour. Skim before using. This makes a useful base for other savoury sauces.

The initial *roux* for this sauce can be made in advance in quantity and will keep in the refrigerator for a long time. Follow the recipe above, using four ounces (100 g) each of butter and flour and omitting the onion. Then when you have to make a brown sauce in a hurry you can simply add the stock and carry on from there.

3 Anchovy Sauce

Time taken: 15–20 mins

½ oz (15 g) butter
½ oz (15 g) flour
½ pint (3 dl) fish stock
(preferably) or milk

lemon juice
1 large teaspoon (approx.)
anchovy essence

Make the white sauce according to the basic recipe (**No 1**) using fish stock instead of milk if you have any available. Add a drop or two of lemon juice and enough anchovy essence to make the sauce a pleasant pink colour. Bring to the boil and stir well.

4 Cheese Sauce

Time taken: 15–20 mins

½ pint (3 dl) white sauce
(**No. 1**)

1 tablespoon grated cheese
1 dessertspoon made mustard

Add the grated cheese to the white sauce, bring to the boil and stir until smooth. Just before using the sauce, add the mustard.

5 Cucumber Sauce
Time taken: 40 mins

1 cucumber
2 oz (50 g) butter
salt and pepper
1 teaspoon flour

1 tablespoon white wine
  vinegar
parsley, chopped

Remove the skin from the cucumber and slice the flesh very thinly, or dice it. Melt the butter in a pan, add the cucumber and cook it gently without burning for about half an hour or until the pieces are soft. Add salt and pepper when the cucumber is half cooked, and when it is soft add the flour previously mixed with the wine vinegar. Sprinkle with parsley before serving. Good with fish.

6 Cream Curry Sauce
Time taken: 20–30 mins

1 oz (25 g) butter
1 onion, finely chopped
1 dessertspoon curry powder
  (or more if liked)

1 oz (25 g) flour
1 pint (6 dl) milk
salt and pepper

Melt the butter in a pan, add the onion and cook until the onion is transparent. Sprinkle in the curry powder and flour and stir well together. Cook for a few minutes, then add the milk. Bring to the boil, season with salt and pepper and simmer for about fifteen minutes.

7 Curry Sauce
Time taken: 1–1½ hours

1 oz (25 g) butter
1 onion, finely chopped
1 tablespoon curry powder
1 oz (25 g) flour
1 apple, finely chopped

1 pint (6 dl) stock
salt
lemon juice
1 oz (25 g) sultanas
1 dessertspoon chutney

Melt the butter, add the onion and cook until the onion is transparent. Sprinkle in the curry powder and flour and cook together for a few moments. Add the apple, the stock and a little lemon juice and season with salt. Bring to the boil, simmer for an hour and before serving add the sultanas and chutney.

8 Egg and Lemon Sauce
Time taken: 10 mins

½ pint (3 dl) chicken or fish
  stock
2 egg yolks

1 lemon
salt and pepper

Heat the stock and add the juice of the lemon. Beat the egg yolks
in a bowl, then pour on to them a little of the hot stock to mix
well, then gradually add the rest. Return the whole to the saucepan
and stir over a gentle heat until it thickens like a custard; take
care not to let it boil or the sauce will curdle. Season if necessary.

This very useful sauce can be served with almost anything. The
liquid used can be varied according to the dish it is to accompany.

9 Herb Gravy
Time taken: 10 mins

Juices from a roast joint
1 glass red wine
2 tablespoons or more fresh
  herbs, chopped

1 teaspoon arrowroot
salt and pepper

Pour off the excess fat from the roasting pan and scrape the juices
into a small saucepan. Pour in the wine and add the herbs. Mix
the arrowroot with a teaspoon of cold water and stir it into the
sauce. Bring to the boil and simmer for a few moments, stirring.
Check the seasoning before serving.

Use the most appropriate herb you have available: mint with
lamb, tarragon with chicken, or parsley with anything.

Mayonnaises
10 Basic Recipe
Time taken: 20 mins

1 egg yolk
1 teaspoon mixed mustard
salt and pepper

sugar if liked
⅓ pint (2 dl) oil
vinegar or lemon juice

Beat the egg yolk with the mustard, a little salt and pepper and,
if liked, a pinch of sugar. Stir in the oil very gradually, first of all
drop by drop, stirring well all the time so that the egg absorbs
the oil. The oil can be added more quickly when the mixture takes
on its thick shiny look, and the addition of the mustard helps to
stop it curdling. If it should curdle, break another egg yolk into

a clean bowl and add the curdled mixture gradually to it, mixing well all the time. Thin as required with a spoonful of vinegar or a few drops of lemon, or a spoonful of cold water.

11 Curried Mayonnaise: Add a tablespoon of curry powder to the finished mixture.

12 Spicy Mayonnaise   Time taken: 20 mins

Add to the finished mayonnaise half a teaspoon of paprika, one or two chopped gherkins, a heaped teaspoon of capers, sufficient tomato purée to give the mixture a pleasant pink colour, and if available, a good teaspoon of Angostura bitters.

13 Mustard Sauce   Time taken: 10 mins

½ oz (15 g) butter   salt and pepper
2–3 teaspoons mustard   paprika
2 teaspoons wine vinegar   2–3 tablespoons cream
½ teaspoon sugar

Melt the butter in a small saucepan and add the mustard. Mix with this the wine vinegar, sugar, salt, black pepper and a little paprika, and finally the cream. Mix well together and use the sauce either hot or cold.

Use English or French mustard according to taste, but it must be a yellow mustard for the sauce to look its best.

14 Onion Sauce (white)   Time taken: 20–30 mins

Boil three onions until soft, then chop them finely and add to a pint of white sauce (**No 1**). Season well and serve hot.

15 Onion Sauce (brown)   Time taken: 20–30 mins

2 or 3 onions, finely chopped   1 pint (6 dl) stock
1 oz (25 g) butter   salt and pepper
1 oz (25 g) flour

Cook the onions gently in the butter until they are soft and beginning to brown. Sprinkle the flour in, mix well and cook until the flour also begins to brown. Add the hot stock gradually, stirring well until it thickens. Season with salt and pepper.

16 Oxford Brawn Sauce   Time taken: 5 mins

1 dessertspoon brown sugar   2 tablespoons vinegar
1 tablespoon mixed mustard   4 tablespoons oil
½ teaspoon salt and pepper

Mix together the mustard, salt, a little pepper, vinegar and oil. Stir well together until smooth.

These proportions can be adjusted at will. This is a very useful sauce as it can be made, then stored in a bottle for future use, and is very good with cold meats.

One of the nicest of the pasta sauces is the herby, garlicky green *pesto* that comes from the region of Genoa, but is not often found in other parts of Italy, and very rarely indeed in this country. It makes an agreeable change from the inevitable *bolognese* or tomato sauce, good though those are. Fresh herbs are essential, and the real sauce is made with fresh basil and pine nuts, but if you haven't either, a good sauce, though quite different in flavour, can be made from parsley and marjoram mixed with walnuts or almonds. It is worth making this sauce in larger quantities than you want immediately as it keeps well, stored in jars with a film of oil over the top, and makes a good instant sauce for pasta or rice; it is also good served instead of butter with baked potatoes.

17 Pesto   Time taken: 25 mins

2 oz (50 g) fresh basil leaves   1 teaspoon salt, pepper,
   (or parsley and marjoram)   2–3 oz (50–70 g) Parmesan
2 teeth garlic   cheese, grated
1 tablespoon pine nuts (or   approx. ¼ pint (1.5 dl) olive oil
   walnuts or almonds)

First chop coarsely the fresh basil leaves, together with the garlic, pine nuts (or almonds or walnuts), the salt and a little pepper. Put this mixture into the blender until it is a soft paste, or pound to the same degree with a pestle and mortar. Gradually add the cheese and work it into the herb paste. Finally add the olive oil, stirred in as if for mayonnaise.

These quantities are sufficient for one pound of spaghetti or other pasta. A mixture of half-and-half Parmesan and Pecorino cheese is even better than Parmesan alone if you can obtain Pecorino.

18 Barbecue Relish   Time taken: 20–25 mins

1 oz (25 g) butter
1 onion, finely chopped
1 lb (450 g) tomatoes, peeled
   or tinned
2 tablespoons vinegar

2 tablespoons demerara sugar
2 tablespoons chutney or
   pickle
Worcestershire sauce
½ teaspoon French mustard

Melt the butter gently in a pan, add the onion and cook for five minutes until it softens (it mustn't brown). Add the tomatoes, vinegar, sugar, chutney or pickle, a dash of Worcestershire sauce, and the French mustard. Mix all these ingredients well together, bring to the boil and simmer for ten minutes. This can be served hot or cold.

Particularly recommended for ham or boiled bacon.

19 Reformed Sauce   Time taken: 1 hour

½ pint (3 dl) brown
   sauce (**No 2**)

1 tablespoon redcurrant jelly
1 glass port

Bring the brown sauce to simmering point, then add the red-currant jelly and port. Stir well until the jelly is melted, bring to the boil and serve hot.

This is based on the famous Reform Sauce, but very much simplified. It is particularly good with meatballs or cutlets.

As a variation use quince jelly, with Madeira or Tarragona instead of port.

20 Salad Dressing (French)   Time taken: 10 mins

salt and pepper
mustard
½ teaspoon sugar, if a
   sweetish dressing is wanted

2 tablespoons vinegar, wine
   for preference
6 tablespoons olive oil

Combine together a teaspoon of salt, a good sprinkling of freshly ground black pepper, a pinch of mustard, the sugar and the vinegar. When this is mixed, add the oil and stir in well.

This can be made in advance, and stored in a bottle. Shake well before using. Garlic or garlic salt can be used if liked, and tarragon vinegar makes a delicious dressing.

21 *Salad Sauce (English)*   Time taken: 25 mins

2 egg yolks	pepper
¼ pint (1.5 dl) thick cream	1 teaspoon water
½ teaspoon salt	1–2 tablespoons vinegar,
1 teaspoon sugar	preferably herb flavoured

Hard boil two eggs, and when cold mash or sieve the yolks into a smooth paste. Mix them with the salt, sugar, pepper and water. When this is well amalgamated, gradually add the cream, stirring well so that the sauce remains smooth, and finally add the vinegar.

This is a lighter and less hazardous sauce to make than mayonnaise, and can be used as an alternative in most dishes. Oil can be used instead of the cream, but this makes the sauce heavier.

22 *Savoury Sauce for Fish*   Time taken: 20–25 mins

1½ oz (40 g) butter	1 dessertspoon Angostura
1 onion, finely chopped	bitters
⅓ pint (2 dl) dry cider or	1 tablespoon lemon juice
white wine	1 heaped tablespoon parsley
1 dessertspoon anchovy	salt and pepper
essence	

Melt the butter in a pan and in it cook the onion until it is soft but not brown. Add all the other ingredients and season with a pinch of salt and pepper. Bring this to the boil and cook rapidly for about ten minutes until the sauce is reduced and slightly thickened.

23 Spaghetti Sauce   Time taken: 30–40 mins

3–4 rashers bacon
1 large onion
1–2 carrots
1 stick celery, if available
1 tablespoon olive oil
1 glass wine

1 small tin tomato purée
1 tooth garlic, finely chopped
salt and pepper
1 teaspoon sugar
½ pint (3 dl) stock or water

Mince the bacon, add the onion, carrots, and celery. Heat the oil in a saucepan, add the bacon and fry for a minute or two, then add the vegetables and cook until the onion begins to look transparent. Add wine and tomato purée, and the garlic, salt, pepper and sugar. Stir well together, then add the stock or water. Cook, uncovered, stirring occasionally, until all the ingredients are soft and the sauce thick.

24 Sweet-Sour Sauce   Time taken: 15 mins

¼ pint (1.5 dl) cider
1 tablespoon brown sugar
1 tablespoon redcurrant jelly

1 tablespoon soy sauce
1 tablespoon cornflour
3 tablespoons vinegar

Bring to the boil the cider, sugar, redcurrant jelly and soy sauce. Mix a tablespoon of cornflour with a little water until smooth, then add it to the cider mixture. Bring to the boil again and simmer for five minutes. Then add the vinegar and stir well.

Serve hot or cold with pork or sausages.

25 Tomato Sauce   Time taken: 20 mins

1 onion, finely chopped
1 tooth garlic, finely chopped
1 tablespoon olive oil
1 bayleaf, if available

1 sprig thyme, if available
1 tin tomatoes
salt and pepper

Cook the onion and garlic gently in the oil until transparent. Add the bayleaf and thyme. Add the tomatoes, chopped or put through a Mouli if you prefer a smoother sauce. Season well with salt and pepper and cook slowly until the sauce is the desired consistency. For a really smooth sauce, put into the blender before serving.

Soups

SOME OF THE SOUPS in this chapter are light, and suitable as a first course with a more substantial dish to follow. Others, such as lentil soup or thick vegetable soups are almost a meal in themselves, and need only cheese and salad or fruit to follow to make a good and satisfying family meal. They are particularly good, too, for the occasions such as a late supper after a theatre when something hot is comforting, as they can be made early in the day and heated through when needed.

Some soups are not made from any recipe, and are never the same twice running, as they depend on using left-over vegetables or meat, put through the ever-useful Mouli or the blender. Sometimes they are the most successful soups of all.

When soups call for stock, vegetable water or a stock cube can be used, or tomato purée diluted with water. For the thicker vegetable soups milk is recommended; if you have no fresh, very good results are obtained from Long Life or powdered milk.

Croutons of crisp fried bread make a good contrast to a bland creamy soup, or vegetable soups can have grated cheese sprinkled over to add a little extra taste and nourishment.

Sometimes home-made soups (and stews too) can be rather pallid. Home-made caramel will give an appetising colour without altering the flavour. Although it is made with sugar, the great heat burns off the sweetness. Dissolve four ounces of sugar in a heavy saucepan over a low heat until it is liquid. Stir occasionally and let it become a dark smoky brown, but take care it doesn't bubble over and burn you. Remove from the heat and allow to cool down. Add, very slowly at first, a quarter pint of hot water, stirring so that the sugar liquefies into it. Be careful doing this as the sugar can burn you so badly. Allow it to get quite cold, then put it into a screw-top bottle for use when wanted. It will keep almost indefinitely.

26 *Apple Soup*   Time taken: 20–30 mins

2 pints (1.2 litres) stock
(made from 2 cubes if
necessary)
1 lb (450 g) cooking apples,
peeled, cored and sliced

1 teaspoon curry powder
½ teaspoon mace
salt
1 oz (25 g) rice or pasta

Bring the stock to the boil and add the apples. Cook gently until
the apple is soft enough to be put through a sieve easily. Return
to the saucepan and add the curry powder, mace and a little salt.
Add the rice or pasta to the soup, simmer until cooked, and serve
the soup very hot.

This has an unusual refreshing sharp taste.

27 *Buchanan Carrot Soup*   Time taken: 40 mins

1 large or 2 small onions,
chopped
1 lb (450 g) carrots, chopped
1½ oz (40 g) butter

1 pint (6 dl) stock or water
salt and pepper
1 teaspoon curry powder

Melt the butter in a saucepan and stir the vegetables in this until
the onion looks transparent. Add the stock or water, season with
salt and pepper and simmer gently until the carrots are quite
soft. Put the mixture through the blender or Mouli until smooth
and stir in a teaspoon of curry powder. Let the mixture simmer
again for another ten minutes.

28 *Barley Soup*   Time taken: 10 mins
preparation; 2 hours cooking

2 onions, chopped
3–4 carrots, chopped
1 stick celery, if available,
chopped
1 turnip, if available, chopped
2 oz (50 g) butter
1 bayleaf

salt and pepper
2 oz (50 g) pearl barley,
soaked, beforehand if
possible
1 dessertspoon tomato purée
soy sauce

Sweat the vegetables for a few moments in the butter. Cover with cold water, add the bayleaf, salt, pepper, pearl barley, tomato purée and a good shake of soy sauce. Bring to the boil and cook gently until all the vegetables are soft, which may take two hours, though if you have time to soak the barley beforehand, this should cut down the cooking time.

This substantial soup is an anglicised version of minestrone, and can be made with whatever vegetables there are to hand. If there are any bones available, add those too.

29 Chestnut Soup   Time taken: 15 mins

1 tin unsweetened chestnut purée
1½ pints (9 dl) beef stock, made from two cubes if necessary

salt and pepper
1 teaspoon mace or nutmeg
cream if desired

Mash up the chestnut purée and gradually add the stock, beating until you get a smooth mixture, or whisk it in the blender if you prefer. Season with salt, pepper, mace or nutmeg. Bring to the boil for a few moments and serve hot. If you like, add a little cream before serving.

A very quick and easy soup with an intriguing flavour. It is meant to be made with boiled chestnuts (you would need about 1 lb (450 g) fresh chestnuts) but it can be made quite successfully with tinned chestnut purée.

30 Egg and Lemon Soup   Time taken: 20 mins

1½ pints (9 dl) chicken stock
2 oz (50 g) rice
1 lemon

salt and pepper
2 egg yolks

Bring the chicken stock to the boil then throw in the rice and cook until the rice is tender. Add the juice of the lemon and adjust the seasoning. Beat the egg yolks in a bowl, then carefully add a few spoonfuls of the hot stock to them, stirring well. Add this mixture to the hot stock in the saucepan and stir well until the mixture thickens. Do not let it boil. Serve as soon as possible.

This is made in a similar way to the egg and lemon sauce (**No 8**) and care must be taken that the soup does not curdle. To avoid this, do not let the soup boil once the eggs have been added.

31 *Green Soup*   Time taken: 30–40 mins

1 onion, finely chopped
1½ oz (40 g) butter
1 large bunch parsley or
 watercress, roughly chopped
1 or 2 potatoes, peeled and
 quartered

salt and pepper
water
1 pint (6 dl) milk
1 egg yolk

Melt the butter in a pan and cook the onion in this. Add the parsley or watercress and turn it in the butter, together with the potatoes. Season with salt and pepper and add sufficient water just to cover. Put the lid on the pan and simmer gently until the potatoes are soft. Put the soup through a Mouli or blender when you should have a thickish purée. Add about a pint of milk so that the soup is rather thinner than you want the finished product to be. Check the seasoning and a few minutes before serving add the beaten yolk of an egg to thicken – it is wise to add a little of the hot soup to the yolk before putting it into the soup. Serve the soup hot, but do not let it boil after the egg has been added. Garnish with a few watercress leaves, or some chopped parsley.

32 *Lentil Soup*   Time taken: 1 hour (less
                                    if lentils pre-soaked)

1½ oz (40 g) butter
1 onion, chopped
1 or 2 carrots, diced
8 oz (225 g) lentils
1 bayleaf

bacon rinds, if available
2 pints (12 dl) water
salt and pepper
milk

Melt the butter in a saucepan and soften in this the onion and carrots. Add the lentils, the bayleaf, and a few bacon rinds. Cover with two pints of cold water, season with salt and pepper and simmer, covered, for about three-quarters of an hour, or until all the vegetables are tender. Put this through the blender and adjust to the required consistency by adding milk. Check the seasoning before serving.

There is no need to soak lentils beforehand, as they will cook quite easily.

33 Mushroom Soup
Time taken: 30 mins

8 oz (225 g) mushrooms, fresh (preferably) or tinned, coarsely chopped

1 medium onion, finely chopped
2 oz (50 g) butter
milk or stock

Melt the butter and sauté the onion in this. Add the mushrooms and pour in just enough water to come nearly to the top of the vegetables. Season well, cover the pan and cook until the vegetables are tender, and the water almost disappeared. Put this mush through the blender and bring to the required consistency with stock or milk. Check the seasoning before serving.

34 Brown Onion Soup
Time taken: 30 mins

3 or 4 onions, diced
1 oz (25 g) butter
salt

1 pint (6 dl) stock
1 tablespoon flour

Melt the butter in a pan and add the onion, turning the pieces thoroughly in the butter so that they become well impregnated. Add a sprinkling of salt, cover the pan and cook for about ten minutes so that the onion becomes soft but not coloured. Sprinkle in the flour and let this take colour slightly, then add the stock. Let the soup cook until the onions are quite soft, which will be in about fifteen minutes.

35 White Onion Soup
Time taken: 30 mins

Make as above, but do not let the onions or flour take colour, and use milk instead of stock for the liquid. A bayleaf can be added with advantage, and this soup is rather nicer put through the blender than served with the bits in.

36 Potato Soup

Time taken: 30 mins

1 lb (450 g) potatoes, peeled
    and quartered
salt and pepper
milk or cream

butter
mace
parsley, chopped

Put the potatoes in a pan with water to cover and season with
salt. Cover the pan and cook until the potatoes are soft enough to
go through the Mouli or blender, together with the cooking
water. Add sufficient milk or cream to bring the soup to the
required consistency, add a lump of butter, a pinch of mace and
pepper and serve very hot sprinkled with parsley and accompanied
by croutons.

37 Potage Crécy

Time taken: 20 mins

1 onion, chopped
2 large carrots, chopped
2 potatoes, chopped

butter
1½ pints (9 dl) water
salt and pepper

Melt the butter in a pan and add the vegetables, stirring them
round so that they get well covered in the butter, and cook for a
few moments without colouring. Add the water, salt and pepper,
cover the pan and cook until all the vegetables are soft enough
to be put through the Mouli together with the cooking liquid.
Stir in a knob of butter and serve hot.

38 Tomato Soup

Time taken: 30 mins

1 large onion, thinly sliced
1 lb (450 g) fresh tomatoes,
    skinned, or 1 tin tomatoes
    oil

1 bayleaf
1 tooth garlic
salt and pepper
1 pint (6 dl) water

Sauté the onions in a little oil until they begin to get soft. Add
the tomatoes, the bayleaf, the garlic, salt, pepper and the water.
Cook with the pan covered until all the ingredients are soft, then
put through the Mouli, removing the bayleaf first. Add more
water if necessary and serve hot or cold. If you want a thicker

soup, use milk instead of water, and butter instead of oil to begin with.

This can be made with fresh or tinned tomatoes, but unless tomatoes are very ripe the tinned ones have more flavour.

39 Madeira Tomato Soup with Egg

Time taken: 20–30 mins

3 onions, finely sliced
3 tablespoons oil
1 lb (450 g) tomatoes, skinned
 chopped and de-seeded *or*
 1 lb tin tomatoes
1 bayleaf
1 tooth garlic, crushed

marjoram or thyme
½ pint (3 dl) water
salt and pepper
4 slices white bread, diced
oil for frying
4 eggs

Cook the onions gently in the oil. Add the tomatoes to the onion with the bayleaf, garlic, a sprinkling of marjoram or thyme, and the water. Season with salt and pepper. Cook until the vegetables are soft, then blend them to a thick purée. Fry the bread cubes until they are crisp, and poach the eggs. Put the fried croutons into the bottom of a soup bowl, cover them with the vegetable purée and put the poached egg on top.

40 Vegetable Soup (1)

Time taken: 30–40 mins

1½–2 lb (675–900 g)
 vegetables, as available, cut
 into thin strips
1 oz (25 g) melted butter

1 teaspoon salt, pepper
1½ pints (9 dl) water
1 dessertspoon tomato purée,
 if liked

Melt the butter in a pan and turn the vegetable pieces in it. Add the salt and pepper and water, with the tomato purée if you like it. Simmer with the lid on the pan until all the vegetables are tender, about half an hour. Check the seasoning.

Use whatever vegetables you have at hand – onion, carrot, potato, turnip, celery, leek, parsnip – the greater the variety the better.

41 *Vegetable Soup (2)*   Time taken: 30–40 mins

1½–2 lb (675–900 g)
  vegetables, as available, cut
  into chunks
1 oz (25 g) butter
salt and pepper
1 bayleaf

1 tooth garlic, if liked
water
milk
1 egg yolk, if wanted
parsley, chopped

Turn the vegetable pieces in the melted butter, add salt, pepper and a bayleaf, garlic if you like, and just cover with water. Cook with the pan covered until you can make the vegetables into thick purée, then adjust to the required consistency with milk. If you want a thick soup, add an egg yolk just before serving, but do not let the mixture boil after this. Sprinkle with parsley, and serve with croutons.

This soup also uses a variety of vegetables, but they are puréed.

42 *Simple Soup*   Time taken: 10 mins

½ pint (3 dl) plain yogurt
½ pint (3 dl) tomato juice,
  (see recipe)
salt and pepper

1 orange
2 or 3 mint leaves
parsley, chopped

Mix together the yogurt and the tomato juice. If you have no tomato juice, sieve the contents of a small tin of tomatoes and bring up to the required amount with water. Add a little salt, pepper, the juice of the orange and the mint leaves. Put all these into the blender until well mixed and taste for seasoning – if the orange is very sweet, add a little lemon juice. Chill well before serving sprinkled with chopped parsley.

This soup and the one that follows make good summery first courses, and are very quick and easy. The tomato soup on page 31 can also be served cold.

B

43 Cucumber and Mint Soup   Time taken: 10 mins

½ pint (3 dl) plain yogurt
¼ pint (1.5 dl) water
1 cucumber, peeled and cut
  into small dice or strips
salt

1 tooth garlic, crushed, if
  liked
1 good tablespoon mint
  leaves, chopped

Beat the yogurt until smooth and thin with the water. Mix in the cucumber, add a little salt, and crushed garlic if you like, and the mint leaves. Chill thoroughly before serving.

Hors d'œuvres

THERE ARE TWO great advantages in serving hors d'œuvres, however simple. One is that while a two course meal remains a family affair, add a third course and it is fit for 'company'.

The other is that if the main dish is rather meagre or make-shift, by giving your family or friends something to eat beforehand the dish goes further as the edge is taken off their appetites.

I have given a few suggestions for hors d'œuvres both hot and cold, but there are innumerable other ideas depending on what you happen to have available: cooked haricot beans (or tinned ones at a pinch); tuna fish; olives; slices of salami or cheese; eggs in all shapes and forms; sardines; left-over vegetables served cold in a dressing. All these in whatever combination you choose serve a useful and delicious purpose.

44 Grapefruit and Mint Salad   Time taken: 10 mins

2 grapefruit
fresh mint, chopped

cucumber, if available,
shredded

Peel the grapefruit and with a sharp knife remove the segments by cutting towards the centre between the membranes. Put the segments into individual bowls and sprinkle with the mint and a little cucumber.

45 Hors d' œuvres

Very satisfactory hors d'œuvres can be made from simple ingredients such as sliced hard-boiled eggs; sardines; sliced tomatoes; any kind of salami sausage sliced; mushrooms sliced and marinaded in a vinaigrette dressing; cold potato salad. Serve them either on individual dishes or arranged on a large platter.

46 Talatouri
Time taken: 15 mins

1 cucumber, sliced or
  shredded
5 fl oz (140 ml) plain yogurt
salt

1 tooth garlic, crushed
1 teaspoon lemon juice
fresh mint, chopped
fresh parsley, chopped

Mix the cucumber with yogurt which has been seasoned with a
little salt and garlic, and with lemon juice if you like. Sprinkle the
mint and parsley over the mixture, and chill well before serving.

This is similar to the cold cucumber soup (**No 43**) except that it
is thicker in consistency.

47 Stuffed Tomatoes
Quick

Tomatoes, like eggs, can be used as containers for a variety of
fillings. They need to be firm and large. Cut off the top of the
tomatoes, scoop out the seeds and the hard centre and fill with
any of the following:

chopped hard-boiled egg mixed with mayonnaise
flaked tuna fish, or other tinned fish such as sardines or salmon
chopped cooked vegetables cut into dice and moistened with
  mayonnaise or vinaigrette
cold cooked rice with sultanas mixed with vinaigrette

The fillings should be moist and well-seasoned.

48 Tomatoes with Eggs
Quick

Cut large tomatoes into slices that do not quite sever the fruit
through, then open the slices like a toast-rack. Between each slice
put a round of hard-boiled egg, and serve on a bed of green
salad.

49 Pâté Maison
Time taken: 10 mins

1 12½ oz (340 g) tin corned
  beef
1 oz (25 g) butter
1 tablespoon sherry or
  Madeira

1 teaspoon parsley, chopped
Worcestershire sauce or
  Angostura bitters

Put the corned beef into the mixer bowl, and mash it up with the butter, sherry or Madeira, chopped parsley and a dash of Worcestershire sauce or Angostura bitters.

Any tinned pâté can also be treated this way, and it makes a good first course served with hot toast.

50 Cream Cheese Mousse

Time taken: preparation 15 mins; setting time 1 hour

8 oz (225 g) Philadelphia cheese
1 tin consommé

1 teaspoon (or more) curry powder

Beat the Philadelphia cheese until smooth with two-thirds of the consommé. Flavour with the curry powder. Fill small ramekins with the mixture, then pour the remaining consommé over in a thin layer. Put in the refrigerator for an hour or so to get really cold and for the mixture to set.

51 Stuffed Eggs

Time taken: 15–20 mins

There are many variations of this simple dish; here are some using ingredients you should usually have at hand.

Hard-boil an egg for each person. Cool quickly in cold water and remove the shells. Cut each egg in half lengthways and carefully remove the yolk. Put the yolks in a bowl and mash up with any of the following:

a teaspoon of mayonnaise to moisten and a little anchovy essence
chopped fresh herbs and a little butter and seasoning
grated cheese and mayonnaise
chopped capers, moistened with a vinaigrette dressing
butter and a teaspoon of curry powder

When the yolks are well mixed, replace the mixture in the whites and serve either on rounds of very crisp fried bread, or garnished with tomato and lettuce.

52 Fish Pâté
Time taken: 10 mins

1 tin pilchards or sardines in tomato sauce

1 slice bread, about 1 inch (2.5 cm) thick
lemon juice, if needed

Remove the backbones from the fish and mash them to a paste in a bowl. Soak the bread in water for a minute, then squeeze it dry and add it to the fish – this gives bulk to the pâté and helps to absorb the oily liquid. Check the seasoning, and if too bland add a little lemon juice. Pile on to a dish and serve with hot toast.

Any tinned fish can be used for this, but pilchards or sardines in tomato sauce are particularly good.

Hot First Courses

53 Grilled Grapefruit
Time taken: 10 mins

grapefruit
demerara sugar

butter
Angostura bitters

Cut the grapefruit in half and cut round and between the segments so they can be removed easily. Sprinkle the top with a little demerara sugar, a tiny piece of butter and three or four drops of Angostura. Put under a hot grill until the butter and sugar melt and the edges of the grapefruit begin to brown.

54 Tomatoes Stuffed with Rice

Allow one tomato for each person. Cut the tomatoes in half and scoop out the pips and the hard core. Fill the centres with cooked well-seasoned rice and bake in a medium oven for fifteen minutes

55 Tomatoes Stuffed with Scrambled Egg

Prepare the tomatoes as above and bake in the oven on a buttered dish for about fifteen minutes. Scramble some eggs (one for each tomato) and when the tomatoes are cooked, fill them with the eggs and serve at once.

56 'A Nice Whet Before Dinner' Time taken: 20 mins

2 slices white bread	1 oz (25 g) grated Cheshire
2 tablespoons oil	cheese
4 anchovy fillets	parsley
	butter

In 1769 Elizabeth Raffald published *The Experienced English Housekeeper*, and this is one of the recipes from it, given as it appears in the book.

Cut some slices of bread half an inch thick, fry them in butter, but not too hard, then split some anchovies, take out the bones, and lay half an anchovy on each piece of bread, have ready some Cheshire cheese grated, and some chopped parsley mixed together, lay it pretty thick over the bread, baste it with butter, and brown it with a salamander; it must be done on the dish in which you send it to table.

It is very good like this, but I prefer to fry the bread in oil as it is crisper, and nowadays we should use anchovy fillets which are already boned. If you think they might be too salty, soak them for half an hour in milk before using them. Not many people have a salamander, but a hot grill is just as good.

Vegetables

WHAT VEGETABLES ARE available in the house at any one time depends to a great extent on whether they are home-grown or not. There is little problem in providing a meal at any time if there is a well-stocked kitchen garden outside and nothing is nicer, whatever frozen food fanciers may say, than freshly picked vegetables cooked straight away. But not all of us can achieve a garden, so on the whole in this section I have confined myself to recipes for the run-of-the-mill vegetables that are obtainable for most of the year, and which are not highly perishable. Root vegetables are particularly good keepers, and potatoes, onions and tomatoes should always be in stock. Cabbage, celery and Chinese leaves also keep for several days in the refrigerator and can be used as a vegetable or a salad.

Some of the dishes can be used as a main course, particularly the potato ones, others are an accompaniment to another dish. A very ordinary main dish can be smartened up considerably by an accompaniment of good vegetables – *Pommes Anna* for instance, although just potatoes and butter, are very different from plain boiled or mashed potatoes. Large onions or potatoes, small marrows and cabbage leaves can all be stuffed to make a satisfying dish. If baking potatoes for stuffing, thread them on to a skewer. They will cook more quickly and evenly.

Cabbage, that much maligned vegetable, bringing with it sad memories of school or boarding house, can be delicious and versatile in use. It seems to have come into favour again though, as it is the favourite vegetable of many school children I know including my own son, who feels that no meal is really complete without cabbage in some form or another.

If vegetables are rather coarse or overgrown, not 'garden-fresh' or 'dew-picked' or whatever evocative phrase advertisers can tempt us with, one way to use them successfully is to make them into a purée, which keeps the flavour but breaks down the coarseness. Root vegetables are very good this way, just as they are, put through the Mouli – one of the most useful gadgets in the kitchen – but green vegetables, such as sprouts or peas, are improved by the addition of a potato or so to give body to the purée, which otherwise may be rather watery. For small amounts of vegetables for flavouring other dishes, the dried vegetables, particularly onions, peppers and freeze-dried peas are excellent, as are dried mushrooms which have a good strong flavour.

Left-over cooked vegetables can be used in several ways. Root vegetables are very good if mashed into a purée, mixed with an egg, formed into cakes and fried up to eat with a meat dish. Green vegetables can be fried up with mashed potatoes into bubble-and-squeak. If there are sufficient vegetables left – and it is almost worth while cooking extra in the first place – put them into a shallow dish, cover them with a cheese or curry sauce, top them with breadcrumbs and brown under a hot grill. Left-over potato can be mashed, mixed with a little flour, seasoned with any available herbs, and fried as potato cakes.

Tinned vegetables can also be dressed up to make them more substantial or more exciting. Spinach is improved by a little cream and nutmeg, and is delicious with a poached or soft-boiled egg, or cheese. Tinned *petits pois* can have diced ham or salami added to them, or one or two tiny onions and a few lettuce leaves, for instant *'petits pois à la française'*. Tinned new potatoes can be drained, dried and sliced, and are then delicious fried in a little oil and butter with plenty of seasoning.

57 Casseroled Carrots

Time taken: preparation 10 mins; cooking 45 mins

1 lb (450 g) carrots, coarsely grated
1½ oz (40 g) butter
salt and pepper

1 teaspoon sugar
3 or 4 tablespoons water
1 teaspoon parsley, chopped

Preheat the oven to 350°F/180°C/Regulo 4. Put the carrots into a well-buttered casserole and season with salt, pepper and sugar.

Add the water and dot with the remaining butter. Cover the casserole and bake in the oven for three-quarters of an hour. Sprinkle with parsley before serving in the casserole.

This is a good way of using carrots that are rather large or coarse, and economical if you are using the oven for cooking the main dish as they can be cooking at the same time, and do not need any attention or come to harm by being over-cooked.

58 Carrots à la Crème   Time taken: 20–30 mins

1 lb (450 g) carrots, scraped
  or peeled
¼ pint water
salt

1 oz (25 g) butter
1 egg yolk
2 fl oz (50 g) cream
1 teaspoon parsley, chopped

If the carrots are small leave them whole, if large cut them into rings. Cook them in a covered pan in the salted water with half the butter added. Turn them once or twice in this and cook until the water has been absorbed. Mix together the egg yolk and cream, and when the carrots are cooked pour this mixture into the pan. Add the other half ounce of butter and the parsley, stir well together, and serve as soon as possible.

59 Buttered Carrots   Time taken: 20–30 mins

1 lb (450 g) carrots, scraped
  or peeled
1 oz (25 g) butter, or more
1 teaspoon sugar

salt
2 tablespoons cream
croutons of fried bread

Cut the carrots, into quarters and boil them gently in salted water until soft. Drain them well and put them through the Mouli to make a thick purée. Return this to the saucepan and let it dry out over a gentle heat; then add the butter, sugar and a pinch of salt. When the butter has melted into the purée, add the cream. Serve very hot with small croutons of crisp fried bread, which provide a good contrast to the soft carrots.

60 Colcannon

Time taken: 30 mins

1 lb (450 g) green vegetables (green cabbage or Brussels sprouts)
1 lb (450 g) potatoes

1 leek or 1 small onion, sliced
¼ pint (1.5 dl) milk
salt and pepper
1 oz (25 g) melted butter

Boil the cabbage or Brussels sprouts and potatoes until tender. They can be cooked separately or together. Simmer the leek or onion in a little milk until soft. Put all the vegetables through the coarsest sieve of the Mouli, or chop them up as finely as possible, with any milk not absorbed by the leek or onion. Beat well until it all becomes a pale green mass which should be smooth and dry. Season with salt and black pepper and serve with melted butter poured into a hollow in the top.

This makes a good accompaniment to boiled bacon or sausages, and any left over can be made into little cakes and fried up.

61 Cauliflower Sauté

Time taken: 20–30 mins

1 cauliflower
1 oz (25 g) or more, butter

1 onion, finely chopped
salt

Separate the cauliflower flowerets and boil them in salted water until just soft, taking care not to overcook them. Drain well – if you intend making soup keep the water as a base. Melt the butter in a frying pan and cook the onion in this for a few minutes before adding the almost cooked cauliflower. Let this take colour, then turn the pieces carefully so that they colour lightly on all sides. Lower the heat and let the pieces continue to cook until tender. Sprinkle lightly with salt and serve hot.

62 Cauliflower au Gratin

Time taken: 30 mins

1 cauliflower
1½ oz (40 g) butter
1 oz (25 g) flour

salt and pepper
nutmeg

Cook the cauliflower as in the last recipe and drain well, keeping the water. Make a white sauce with an ounce of the butter using a pint of the cauliflower water as the liquid. Season with salt, pepper and a little nutmeg. Put the cooked cauliflower into an ovenproof dish, cover with the sauce, dot with the remaining butter and brown under a hot grill or in the oven.

63 *Cauliflower Cakes*   Time taken: 20–30 mins

1 cauliflower
salt and pepper
nutmeg

1 teaspoon parsley, if
  available, chopped
1 oz (25 g) butter

Prepare and cook the cauliflower in water until soft. Mash into a purée with a fork, season with salt, black pepper and nutmeg, and add a little chopped parsley, if available. Form this into one large or several small flat cakes with a little butter added, and fry quickly until brown; turn over and brown the other side. If you use a non-stick pan, no fat is necessary to fry them in.

64 *Cauliflower à la Polonaise*   Time taken: 30 mins

1 cauliflower
2 eggs, hard-boiled
1 teaspoon parsley, chopped

2 oz (50 g) breadcrumbs
1 oz (25 g) butter

Remove the outer leaves and hard stalk from the cauliflower and cut it into quarters. Boil these gently in salted water until tender. Meanwhile chop the hard-boiled eggs finely and mix them with the parsley and breadcrumbs. Brown this mixture in a frying pan in the butter. When the cauliflower is cooked, drain it well, put the quarters together to look like a whole cauliflower and sprinkle with the egg-and-breadcrumb mixture.

65 *Sweet-Sour Cabbage*   Time taken: preparation
10 mins; cooking 1 hour

1 lb (450 g) cabbage,
  shredded
2 tablespoons dripping
1 tablespoon sugar
1 onion, finely chopped

1 tablespoon vinegar
salt and pepper
caraway seeds
1 glass white wine or cider

Heat the dripping in a heavy pan, add the sugar and stir until it melts. Add the onion and let this cook for a few minutes, then pour in the vinegar and the shredded cabbage. Season with salt and pepper and a few caraway seeds. Stir well, then add the white wine or cider. Stew the cabbage gently in a covered pan for about an hour when it will be tender and the liquid absorbed.

66 Fried Cabbage   Time taken: 15 mins

1 cabbage, finely shredded	salt and pepper
1 medium onion, chopped	1 teaspoon, cornflour
2 tablespoons oil	2 or 3 tablespoons water

Heat the oil in a heavy frying pan and when hot but not smoking add the onion and cook, stirring well, for two or three minutes. Then add the cabbage and continue to cook and stir for about three minutes. Season with salt and pepper and add the cornflour, mixed with the water to a smooth paste, to the cabbage. Turn the cabbage pieces well and cook for a further three or four minutes, when the pieces should be cooked but still crisp.

This is quickly done, and is best prepared so that it can be served as soon as possible after cooking.

67 Stewed Cabbage   Time taken: 30 mins

1 cabbage, cut into strips	salt and pepper
1 onion, finely chopped	1 teaspoon flour
1 tablespoon oil	lemon juice
1 oz (25 g) butter	cream, if available

Put the cabbage strips into salt water for about fifteen minutes, and meanwhile soften the onion in a mixture of oil and butter. Add the shredded cabbage, cook for five minutes in the fat, then pour on boiling water to cover. Season, put the lid on the pan and simmer until the cabbage is tender. When ready, stir in the flour, adjust the seasoning, add a squeeze of lemon juice and pour in a spoonful or two of cream if available.

68 Stewed Onions

Time taken: 1–1½ hours

4 onions
1½ pints (9 dl) stock

flour (optional)
dripping (optional)

Take the outer skin from four large onions and trim the ends, without cutting into the vegetable itself. Put them into a saucepan in which they fit closely in one layer, cover them with stock and stew them gently in a covered pan for an hour or more according to size, or until they are tender but not falling to bits. The onions can be rolled in flour and lightly browned in dripping before being stewed.

Onions, although invaluable in adding flavour to an enormous variety of dishes, are not greatly used on their own. But this way of serving them as a vegetable is particularly good with roast meat.

69 Onions and Crispy Noodles

Time taken: 25 mins

2–3 onions, sliced into
    thin rings
oil for frying
½ lb (225 g) noodles
    (boiled for 5 mins then
    drained)

milk
flour
salt

Heat a pan half full of oil until hot and fry the noodles in small quantities at a time until crisp; drain well and keep hot. Dip the onion rings in milk and then into flour, shake off the excess, and fry them in the same oil used for the noodles until they are crisp and brown. Drain well on kitchen paper before mixing with the fried noodles. Sprinkle with salt before serving.

70 Potatoes Anna

Time taken: 1–1½ hours

1½ lb (675 g) waxy
    potatoes

2–3 oz (50–75 g) butter
salt

Peel the potatoes and slice them thinly and evenly so that the slices are about the size and thickness of an old penny. This is quickly and easily done if you have a slicer or *mandoline*. Wash the slices, then dry them thoroughly with a cloth or kitchen paper. Butter a fireproof dish well and arrange the potato slices evenly over the bottom of the pan and round the sides in layers, adding a few dabs of butter and a little salt between each layer, until the dish is full. For six layers or so of potatoes you would use about two ounces (50 g) of butter. Put the lid on the dish (if it has no lid, cover closely with foil) and cook gently for about forty-five minutes. Take the lid off the pan and finish the cooking in a hot oven for about ten minutes so that the top gets brown. If you have no suitable dish for this, start the cooking in a frying-pan until the potatoes start to get a little soft, then arrange the slices in a buttered mould and finish them in the oven.

71 *Potato Boulettes*
Time taken: 30 mins

1 lb (450 g) potatoes
1½ oz (40 g) butter
1 teaspoon salt
nutmeg

2 eggs, separated
oil, or oil and butter, for
frying

Boil the potatoes and mash them until they are smooth and dry. Mix them with the butter, salt, a little nutmeg and the egg yolks. Beat up the egg whites until stiff and fold them into the potato mixture. Heat the oil, or mixture of oil and butter, in a pan; form the potato mixture into small balls with a teaspoon, and when the oil is hot drop them into the pan and fry until they are pale brown and swollen. Drain well and serve at once.

72 *Potato Cakes*
Time taken: 15 mins

1 lb (450 g) potatoes, mashed
4 oz (100 g) flour
salt and pepper
nutmeg

garlic, if liked
dripping, or oil and butter for
frying

This is a good way of using up any left-over potato. Add to the smoothly mashed potato sufficient flour to make it into a firm paste – about four ounces. Season well with salt, pepper, nutmeg and garlic if you like. Form into flat cakes and fry quickly in the dripping or the oil and butter until brown on both sides.

73 Potato Dauphinoise
Time taken: 1–1½ hours

1½ lb (675 g) potatoes,
  peeled and thinly sliced
1½ oz (40 g) butter
2 oz (50 g) cheese, preferably
  Gruyère, grated

salt and pepper
mace
1 egg
½ pint (3 dl) milk
garlic, if liked

Preheat the oven to 350°F/180°C/Regulo 4. Butter an ovenproof dish thoroughly and rub the dish with garlic, if liked. Put half the potato slices into the dish, cover this with a layer of grated cheese and season with salt and pepper. Cover with the rest of the potatoes, another layer of cheese, a little mace, salt and pepper. Beat the egg with the milk and pour this over the potatoes in the dish. Dot with the remaining butter and put into the oven for about half an hour. Serve in the dish.

74 Potato Gratinée
Time taken: 25 mins

1 lb (450 g) potatoes, mashed
½ pint (3 dl) milk
2 oz (50 g) butter

1–2 oz (25–50 g) grated
  cheese
salt and pepper

Preheat the oven to 400°F/200°C/Regulo 6. Heat the milk and add it to the mashed potatoes with the salt, an ounce and a half (40 g) of the butter and a tablespoon of the cheese. Put this well-mixed purée into a buttered fireproof dish, sprinkle with the rest of the cheese, dot with butter and put into the oven for about fifteen minutes to brown the top.

This is similar to the previous recipe but made with mashed potatoes.

75 Janssen's Temptation
Time taken: 1 hour

1 tin anchovies
1 onion, sliced into thin rings
1½ oz (40 g) butter

3 medium potatoes, cut into
  matchsticks
¼ pint (1.5 dl) cream

Preheat the oven to 350°F/180°C/Regulo 4, Wash the anchovies in cold water to remove some of the saltiness. Cook the onion rings gently in most of the butter until they soften. Wash and dry the potato sticks. Butter an ovenproof dish and put in half the potatoes, then the onions, followed by the anchovies, which have been dried on kitchen paper, and finally the remainder of the potatoes. Dot with the remaining butter and put into the oven. After ten minutes, pour on half the cream so that it is absorbed by the potatoes, and after a further ten minutes pour on the remainder. Leave the dish to cook for about forty minutes or until the potatoes are soft.

76 Potato Latkes

Time taken: 20–30 mins

1 lb (450 g) potatoes, peeled
1 large onion
3–4 oz (75–100 g) flour

salt and pepper
oil for frying

Grate the potatoes together with the onion. Put them into a mixing bowl with the flour and season well with salt and pepper. Heat some oil in a frying-pan and when hot – but not as hot as you would have for chips – drop in spoonfuls of the potato mixture and fry until brown on both sides. Sometimes an egg is added to the potato–flour mixture, but this tends to make the latkes rather leathery.

77 Potato Lyonnaise

Time taken: 30–40 mins

1½ lb (675 g) potatoes
2 onions, chopped
salt and pepper

2½ oz (65 g) butter
parsley, chopped

Put the potatoes into cold water with salt added, bring them slowly to the boil and let them cook for about twenty minutes. Drain them and when cool enough, cut them into slices. Meanwhile cook the onions in an ounce and a half (40 g) of the butter without browning them. Add the potato slices and the other ounce (25 g) of butter, salt and pepper, and finish cooking until the potatoes and onions are soft. Sprinkle with chopped parsley before serving very hot. The potatoes can be cooked in their skins and then peeled if they are small enough to be cooked whole, which keeps their flavour better.

78 Pan-Roasted Potatoes   Time taken: 40–50 mins

1½ lb (675 g) potatoes, peeled   oil or dripping
stock or water   salt
1 tooth garlic

Boil the potatoes, whole if small, quartered if large, slowly in
stock or in water with a tooth of garlic until they are nearly but
not quite cooked. Drain the potatoes and heat the oil or dripping
in a heavy saucepan. When the fat is hot finish cooking the
potatoes in the pan, turning them from time to time so that they
get browned all over. The outside should be brown and crisp and
the inside soft.

79 Potato Rissoles   Time taken: 30–40 mins

1 lb (450 g) potatoes   breadcrumbs
1 egg, separated   dripping, or oil and butter for
salt and pepper   frying

Boil the potatoes, preferably in their skins, peel them and mash
them to a purée. Mix in the beaten egg yolk and season well with
salt and pepper. When the mixture is cool, make little rolls or
rounds about the size of a large cork. Dip these into the slightly
beaten egg white, then into breadcrumbs and fry in hot dripping
or a mixture of butter and oil until golden.

These are different from the potato cakes (No 72) in that egg
is added but no flour. You can vary them by using crushed
almonds instead of breadcrumbs, or Matzo meal or even semolina;
if you like you can mix one or two raisins into each rissole.

80 Stuffed Potatoes   Time taken: preparation
20 mins; cooking 40 mins

4 large potatoes   4 oz (100 g) cooked ham or
1 oz (25 g) butter   bacon, finely chopped or
1 oz (25 g) flour   minced
¼ pint (1.5 dl) milk   1 oz (25 g) grated cheese
salt and pepper   1 egg yolk
mace or nutmeg

Peel the potatoes and cut them in half lengthwise. Scoop out a hollow from the cut side, and trim a little off the other side so that they will sit steady on a dish. Put them into salted water and bring them to the boil for five minutes, then drain them and let them cool. Make a *roux* with the butter and flour, add the warm milk and cook for five minutes, stirring all the time until the sauce is thick and smooth. Season with salt, pepper and a little mace or nutmeg. Remove from the fire, add the ham or bacon, grated cheese and the egg yolk, and mix well. Put the potatoes on to a well-buttered dish, hollow side up, fill them with the sauce and bake them in a moderate oven for thirty to forty minutes until the potatoes are cooked through.

81 Potato Turnovers
Time taken: 45 mins

1 lb (450 g) mashed potatoes 1 oz (25 g) butter
4 oz (100 g) flour meat for stuffing

Mix the mashed potatoes with the flour and butter. Knead until the mixture becomes a smooth paste that can be rolled out. Roll to about a quarter of an inch thickness, then cut into rounds (I use a six-inch (15 cm) saucepan lid as a cutter). Put some well-seasoned cooked meat, minced or finely chopped, on to one half, then fold over the rest of the paste to make a half circle.

Press the edges together and fry the turnovers in hot fat until they are nicely coloured; drain them well and serve them with gravy or a tomato sauce.

82 Baked Tomatoes
Time taken: 20–25 mins

4 large tomatoes parsley, or any other fresh
salt herb, chopped
garlic, crushed butter or oil

Preheat the oven to 350°F/180°C/Regulo 4. Cut the tomatoes in half and with a sharp knife make one or two cuts across the top of the hard core. Sprinkle with salt, a little garlic and the parsley, or whatever herb you choose. Put a dab of butter on each tomato half, or else moisten with a little oil, put the tomatoes on to a shallow fireproof dish and bake them in the oven for about fifteen minutes.

A variation on this is to put a layer of grated cheese instead of the herbs on to the tomatoes.

83 Scalloped Tomatoes   Time taken: 40–50 mins

1 lb (450 g) tomatoes, skinned
    and sliced
1 onion, finely chopped
2 oz (50 g) butter
2 bacon rashers, diced

2 oz (50 g) grated cheese
2 oz (50 g) soft breadcrumbs
fresh herbs (parsley or
    marjoram or whatever is
    available), chopped

Preheat the oven to 400°F/200°C/Regulo 6. Cook the onion gently in an ounce (25 g) of the butter until soft, adding the bacon for the last minute or two of cooking. Mix the cheese with the breadcrumbs. Butter a fireproof dish and put in a layer of tomatoes, onions and bacon, the fresh herbs and half the cheese and breadcrumb mixture. Then put another layer of vegetables and the remainder of the cheesy breadcrumbs in a thick layer on top, trickle melted butter over this and bake, uncovered, in the oven for half an hour.

84 Tomatoes and Onions   Time taken: 25–30 mins

1 lb (450g) tomatoes, skinned,
    deseeded and quartered
2 large onions, sliced
1 tablespoon oil

1 oz (25 g) butter
1 or 2 teeth garlic, crushed
salt and pepper
parsley, chopped

Cook the onions in a mixture of oil and butter until they begin to look transparent. Add the garlic, put in the tomatoes, season with salt and a little black pepper and cook until the vegetables are soft, adding some chopped parsley just before the cooking is finished.

This is a simplified version of a ratatouille, and makes a good accompaniment to a rather dry dish.

85 Mixed Buttered Vegetables   Time taken: 40 mins

1 small cabbage or ½ lb (225 g)   1 green pepper, if available
   Brussels sprouts   2 oz (50 g) butter
2 carrots   salt
1 or 2 stalks celery   lemon juice

Wash the vegetables and keep them in warm water until you are
ready to slice and cook them. Cut them all into slices, and if you
are using a green pepper take care to remove all the seeds. Melt
the butter in a heavy pan and add the vegetables, mix them well,
add salt and cook them gently in the butter, stirring so that they
do not stick and get brown, for about twenty minutes, or until the
are soft but not mushy. Finally, add a little lemon juice and serve
very hot.

This is particularly good with sausages or pork, or it can be
used as a dish on its own. Use whatever mixture of vegetables you
have at hand.

86 Vegetable Ragoût   Time taken: preparation
                                   20 mins; cooking 30–40 mins

1½–2 lb (645 g–1 kg) mixed   herbs as available
   vegetables (including an   1 tablespoon flour
   onion) prepared and sliced   about ½ pint (3 dl) stock, or 1
1 oz (25 g) butter or bacon   tablespoon tomato purée
   fat   diluted in water
salt and pepper   grated cheese

Melt some butter or bacon fat in a saucepan, add the onion and
cook for a few minutes; then add the rest of the vegetables and
turn them so that they are well coated with the fat. Season with
salt, pepper and any favourite herbs; sprinkle in the flour, mix
well and cover the vegetables with stock or tomato purée diluted
in water. Cover the pan and cook until the vegetables are soft.
Serve hot, with grated cheese.

This can also be made with whatever vegetables are to hand –
a mixture of onion, carrot, cauliflower, peas, swedes, parsnips,
according to availability and season.

87 *Cauliflower Cheese*   Time taken: 30 mins

1 cauliflower   2 tablespoons grated cheese
1 onion, finely chopped   salt and pepper
1 oz (25 g) butter   mace
1 oz (25 g) flour   browned breadcrumbs
1 pint (6 dl) (or less) milk

Break the cauliflower into sprigs and cook in boiling salted water until tender. Cook the onion in the butter until soft, and stir in the flour. Mix in a pint of milk (you can dilute it with some of the cauliflower water) and add a tablespoon of the cheese. Season with salt, pepper and a little mace. Drain the cauliflower and put it into an ovenproof dish; pour the cheese sauce over, sprinkle with the breadcrumbs and the remaining cheese, and heat in the oven or under the grill to brown.

Bacon or boiling sausage make good additions to this. If using bacon, fry it first, either whole or diced, and then fry the onions in the bacon fat with added butter if necessary.

88 *Carrot and Parsley Ring*   Time taken: 1 hour

1 lb (450 g) carrots   2 eggs, separated
1 dessertspoon grated cheese   *for the sauce:*
1 tablespoon chopped parsley   1 oz (25 g) butter
salt and pepper   1 oz (25 g) flour
1½ oz (40 g) butter   ½ pint (3 dl) milk
1 oz (25 g) flour   1 dessertspoon grated cheese
4 tablespoons milk   1 tablespoon chopped parsley

Cook the carrots until they are soft, then mash or blend them to a purée. Stir in the cheese and parsley and season with salt and pepper. Preheat the oven to 400°F/200°C/Regulo 6.

In a small saucepan, melt the butter, stir in the flour and add the milk. Stir and cook until thickened. Add the well-beaten yolks of the eggs, stir well together and mix into the carrots. Beat the egg whites until stiff, then fold them gently into the carrot mixture and pour it into a well-oiled ring mould, or soufflé dish. Put the dish into a pan of hot water to come halfway up the sides of the dish, and bake in the oven for about half an hour. Remove from the oven, wait a few moments, then reverse the mould on to a hot serving dish. Serve with a cheese and parsley sauce. (**No 4**).

For a more substantial dish fill the centre of the mould with cooked cauliflower sprigs, or spinach, or left-over chicken.

89 Vegetables au Gratin
Time taken: 40 mins

1½ lb (675 g) mixed vegetables, washed and prepared
for the sauce:
½ oz (25 g) butter
½ oz (25 g) flour
milk if necessary

either 1 dessertspoon grated cheese
1 teaspoon made mustard
or 1 onion, finely chopped
1 teaspoon curry powder

breadcrumbs *or* grated cheese

Cook a mixture of vegetables as in **No 86** and when they are cooked drain off and reserve any liquid. Make a cheese (**No 4**) or curry (**No 6**) sauce using the liquid from the vegetables, made up to half a pint with milk if needed. Put the cooked vegetables into an ovenproof dish, cover with the sauce, scatter browned breadcrumbs or grated cheese on top, and heat through in a hot oven or brown under the grill.

90 Vegetable Sea Pie
Time taken: preparation 20 mins; cooking 1 hour

1½ lb (675 g) mixed vegetables
1 tablespoon dripping or bacon fat

1 oz (25 g) flour
½ pint (3 dl) stock or water
4 oz (100 g) self-raising flour
2 oz (50 g) suet

Turn the vegetables in the fat, sprinkle with flour, season, pour on stock or water to come halfway up the vegetables, and bring to simmering point. Make a suet crust from the self-raising flour and suet and sufficient water to mix to a dough. Roll the paste out and cut out a circle to fit the saucepan – the easiest way to do this is to use the saucepan lid as the cutter. Any paste left over can be rolled into dumplings and dropped into the simmering vegetables. Put the suet crust on top of the vegetables, replace the saucepan lid and simmer gently for an hour. Preferably serve it in the pan in which it was cooked, otherwise cut the crust into triangles, put them into the middle of the serving dish and place the vegetables round them.

This is made with a similar mixture of vegetables, but is particularly good with a lot of root vegetables in it. To make a more substantial dish add some chopped corned beef.

91 Brussels Sprouts Sauté   Time taken: 30–40 mins

1 lb (450 g) Brussels sprouts,   1 oz (25 g) butter
  washed   salt

Boil the sprouts for about fifteen minutes in salted water in an uncovered pan and drain them well. Heat the butter in a heavy pan, put in the sprouts and finish cooking them in the butter, turning them so that they get lightly browned.

92 Brussels Sprouts and Bacon Time taken: 30–40 mins

1 lb (450 g) Brussels sprouts   lard
2–3 rashers smoked bacon,
  diced

Cook the sprouts, uncovered in salted water for about fifteen minutes. Cook the bacon for a few minutes in a pan, add a little lard if necessary, then put in the sprouts and finish cooking them with the bacon, turning them to take colour on all sides.

93 Fried Brussels Sprouts

Sprouts can be sliced and cooked in the same way as cabbage, see No 66.

94 Brussel Sprouts and Chestnuts

                                    Time taken: 30–40 mins

1 lb (450 g) Brussels sprouts   salt
1 tin chestnut purée   butter
egg yolk

Sprouts and chestnuts go particularly well together, but if you have no chestnuts available a good substitute can be made by using tinned chestnut purée. Cook the sprouts, uncovered, in salted water until almost tender. Mix the chestnut purée with an egg yolk to bind, add a little salt and form into small balls about the size of the sprouts. Finish the sprouts by cooking them in a little butter, add the chestnut balls so that they heat through – but take care when turning them that they do not break – and serve them together with the sprouts.

95 Lentil Ragoût

Time taken: 1–1½ hours

½ lb (225 g) lentils
½ oz (15 g) butter
2–3 rashers fat bacon, diced
1 onion, chopped
1–2 carrots, diced
1 stick celery, chopped

4 oz (100 g) tomatoes, skinned and chopped, or 2–3 tablespoons tomato purée mixed with ¼ pint (1.5 dl) water
salt and pepper
chopped parsley

Soak the lentils for several hours, then drain them. Melt the butter in a casserole, add the fat bacon and cook until the fat begins to run, then add the onion, carrots and celery. Turn them in the butter until they are well coated, then add the drained lentils and stir again so that the mixture is well amalgamated and beginning to take a little colour. Add the tomatoes (or the tomato purée with the water added), salt and pepper. Cover the pan and cook slowly for about an hour and a half. Add a little liquid if it looks as if it is going to dry out, but the finished dish should be thick. Sprinkle with chopped parsley before serving.

This ragoût can be eaten by itself, or as a good accompaniment to sausages or pork rashers.

Any left-overs can be put through the Mouli, moulded into little cakes and fried, to be used instead of potatoes, or served with bacon.

96 Baked Beans

Time taken: soaking overnight;
preparation 20 mins;
cooking overnight

1 lb (450 g) haricot beans
bicarbonate of soda
1 onion, finely chopped
bacon, if available, or bacon
  rinds

2 tablespoons dark treacle
dry mustard
1 teaspoon salt
1 tablespoon tomato purée

Soak the haricot beans in cold water overnight. The next day drain them, cover them with fresh cold water, add a pinch of bicarbonate of soda and bring them to the boil. Cook for about five minutes, then drain and run cold water through the beans. Alternatively, if you are short of time, cover them with cold water, bring them to the boil, turn off the heat and leave them until cool in the water. Add the onion to the beans in a large casserole, together with a piece of bacon if possible, or bacon rinds if that is all there is, two tablespoons of treacle, a little dry mustard and a teaspoon of salt. Cover the beans with cold water, with the tomato purée to give more flavour, put the lid on the pot and cook for several hours until soft. It may be necessary to add a little water after the first hour.

The exact cooking time of this dish depends on how fresh the beans are, but it will take four or five hours minimum. Sometimes it is easier to soak the beans during the day, make up the casserole and leave it all night in a very slow oven. A little over-cooking won't hurt them.

97 Bean and Macaroni Stew

Time taken: preparation
20 mins; cooking 2–2½ hours

8 oz (225 g) haricot or red
  beans
2 tablespoons oil
1 onion, chopped
8 oz (225 g) pork belly,
  fresh or salt
cinnamon

nutmeg
pepper
1 tablespoon tomato purée
3 pints (1.8 litres) water
1 teaspoon salt
2 oz (50 g) short-cut
  macaroni

Warm the oil in as aucepan, then add the beans, the onion and the pork belly. Season with a little cinnamon, nutmeg and pepper, and add the tomato purée and water. Cover the pan and cook gently for about an hour, then add a good teaspoon of salt, cover again and cook for another hour or until the beans are tender. If there is a lot of liquid, cook rapidly for another twenty minutes or so with the lid off the pan so that the liquid reduces. Add the macaroni and simmer, with the lid off the pan, until the macaroni is cooked. Serve very hot, sprinkled with grated cheese if you like. This amount should serve six people.

There is no need to soak the beans beforehand for this dish.

98 Bean Stew

Time taken: preparation
20 mins; cooking 2 hours
(soak beans overnight)

1 lb (450 g) haricot beans
2 onions, diced
2 carrots, diced
1 leek, diced
1 stick celery or celeriac,
   diced

1 tablespoon oil
½ lb (225 g) bacon, chopped
   or in rashers
tomato purée
1 heaped teaspoon paprika
1 dessertspoon salt

Soak the haricot beans overnight, then cook them in the water they soaked in for about two hours, or until they are soft. Fry the onions, carrots, leek and celery or celeriac in the oil, then add them to the beans. Fry the bacon in the same oil, then add it to the beans. Deglaze the pan with hot water and a little tomato purée to improve the colour of the dish, and add this to the beans together with a heaped teaspoon of paprika and a dessertspoon of salt. Continue to cook slowly until the meat and beans are quite cooked, and sprinkle a little parsley over the beans before serving.

99 Curried Butter Beans

Time taken: preparation
20 mins; cooking 2 hours
Soak beans overnight

8 oz (225 g) butter beans
1 tablespoon oil
1 onion, finely chopped
1½ pints (9 dl) stock (made
  from a stock cube if
  necessary)
salt
for the sauce:
1 tablespoon oil

1 onion, finely chopped
1 heaped tablespoon curry
  powder
1 tablespoon flour
1 apple, peeled and thinly
  sliced
1 oz (25 g) sultanas
salt and pepper

Soak the beans overnight or for several hours. Heat the oil in a large saucepan and soften the onion in this without letting it brown. Stir in the drained beans, mixing them well with the onion and oil. Add the stock, bring slowly to the boil and simmer gently until the beans are soft – this may take an hour and a half to two hours, depending on the beans. Add salt after they have been cooking for about half an hour. When the beans are cooked, strain off the liquid and reserve it for the sauce.

To make the sauce, heat the oil and cook the onion in it, then stir in the curry powder and let this cook for about five minutes. Add the flour, cook for a minute or two, then add the liquid in which the beans were cooked. Bring to the boil, stirring well so that it doesn't burn. Add the apple and sultanas to the sauce, season with salt and pepper and simmer for half an hour until the sauce is thickened. Stir in the cooked beans, heat them through thoroughly and serve very hot.

This dish should be accompanied by poppadums and chutney. A crisp salad such as celery, chicory or, best of all, Chinese leaves, also goes well with it. You can serve rice as well if you wish, but the textures are too similar to be ideal.

100 Barley Rissoles

Time taken:
soak barley in preparation
cooking 1–1½ hours

4 oz (100 g) pearl barley
½ pint (3 dl) or more stock or
   water
salt and pepper
1 onion, finely diced
1 oz (25 g) butter

1 oz (25 g) bacon or ham,
   finely chopped (if liked)
1 oz (25 g) flour
chopped parsley
egg and breadcrumbs
oil for frying

Wash the pearl barley and soak it in water overnight. Drain it, then put it into a saucepan with the stock and season with salt and pepper. Cover the pan and simmer until the stock is absorbed and the barley quite soft – you may have to add more liquid from time to time. Drain the barley and set it aside, reserving any liquid. Cook the onion gently in the butter until soft, adding the bacon or ham. Stir in the flour and the liquid in which the barley was cooked, making up the amount with milk if necessary. When the sauce is thickened, add the barley and season well with salt, pepper and parsley.

Leave the mixture to cool, then form it into rissoles; dip them into beaten egg, then breadcrumbs and fry them in hot oil until brown. They should be crisp outside and soft within. Serve very hot, accompanied by tomato or cheese sauce.

Salads

VEGETABLES DO NOT have to be served hot to be good – almost any vegetable, cooked or raw, can be made into a salad. Apart from the more obvious 'summery' ones like tomatoes, lettuce and so on, the hard white cabbage, or grated carrot or turnip are good when served in a flavoury dressing, and plainly cooked vegetables that are left over from one meal can be allowed to go cold, dressed and used as a side salad or as part of a mixed hors d'œuvres. Dried vegetables such as lentils or beans also make good and filling salads, and with a couple of hard-boiled eggs served on a bed of lightly curried rice any salad makes a good meal.

Here are a few suggestions for dishes using the ingredients likely to be around the house – others using chicory, peppers and more exotic vegetables can be used in similar ways according to their availability.

One of the most useful and delicious vegetables now fairly widely available are Chinese cabbages. They come from Israel, and are in season from about November until the summer, with a short break in April, and although they may seem expensive – they are sold by weight – they keep very well in a refrigerator, can be cooked like celery, or a few stalks make one of the crispest and most satisfying salads I know, without any of the bitterness of chicory or the rather assertive taste of celery. Just use as many stalks as needed and put the rest back into the refrigerator for further use, and one bunch of these leaves will keep the family in salad for about a week.

101 Green Salad

Wash and shake dry the green salad and put it into the bowl. Sprinkle with salt and pour on one or two tablespoons of oil and mix the salad well with the oil so that it all gets a good coating. Then sprinkle on a few drops only of vinegar and mix again. This way the oil protects the leaves from becoming sodden with the vinegar and the salad remains much more crisp.

This is particularly for green salads which can so often be too soggy or vinegary.

102 Cabbage Salad
Time taken: 10–15 mins

1 lb (450 g) hard white cabbage, very finely shredded or grated

2–3 carrots, shredded or grated

1 small onion, if liked, very finely, chopped

1 apple, peeled and diced, *or* handful of sultanas

3–4 tablespoons oily French dressing

Mix all the vegetables together, add the apple or sultanas and pour the dressing over them. Mix thoroughly so that all the salad is well coated, then put into a bowl in the refrigerator with a weighted saucer on top, and leave for at least two hours, overnight if possible.

103 Carrot Salad
Time taken: 10 mins

3–4 carrots, scraped and coarsely grated

2 stalks celery, diced, *or* half a cucumber, grated

1 apple, diced

1 tablespoon parsley, chopped

French dressing

Mix the vegetables together and add the apple and parsley. Turn this mixture in plenty of French dressing, as it will absorb quite a lot, and leave it in a cool place until ready to serve.

104 Dandelion Salad

8 dandelion plants
2 slices of bread, diced
2 diced bacon rashers

oil
salt
vinegar

Clean, wash and drain the dandelion plants, and trim off the roots just below the leaves. Blanch them for a few seconds if you like. Sauté the bacon until the fat runs, then add the bread and fry that in the fat, adding a little oil. When the bread and bacon are cooked and crisp, drain well, add the dandelions, and sprinkle with salt and a few drops of vinegar.

Surely the most economical salad of all, for even the smallest garden patch is likely to have one or two plants lurking somewhere. Pick them when the plants are young for preference, or they develop a bitter taste.

105 Dubarry Salad

1 cauliflower
1 small onion, finely chopped
parsley

vinaigrette dressing
2 hard-boiled eggs, quartered

Divide the cauliflower into sprigs and cook them in salted water until just tender, but not mushy. Mix the cauliflower and onion, sprinkle with parsley and turn in a vinaigrette dressing. Garnish with the egg quarters.

106 Tomato Salad

5 or 6 tomatoes; skinned or
   not, as liked
salt and black pepper
1 teaspoon onion, finely
   chopped

1 tablespoon fresh herbs as
   available (parsley,
   marjoram or tarragon)
2–3 tablespoons oil

Cut the tomatoes into four or five slices, according to their size, and put the slices on a plate; sprinkle with salt and leave for about half an hour, then drain off any liquid that will have come from them. Put a very small quantity of chopped onion into the salad bowl, add the tomato slices, sprinkle well with whatever fresh herb you have, such as parsley, marjoram or tarragon, and black pepper and pour over the whole two or three tablespoons of oil.

This is one of the best and simplest of salads, good as a first course or with a cold main dish. The tomatoes must be firm, and can be skinned or not as you please. My own preference is for skinning them, which is easily done by plunging them into boiling water for a few moments.

107 Tomato Jelly

Time taken: 30 mins
Make in advance

1 lb (450 g) tomatoes, skinned, or 1 tin tomatoes
1 onion, chopped
1 bayleaf
1 or 2 stalks celery, or 1 teaspoon celery salt

1 dessertspoon sugar
½ teaspoon salt
paprika
½ oz (15 g) gelatine
1 tablespoon wine or tarragon vinegar

Chop the tomatoes fairly small and put them in a saucepan with the onion, bayleaf, celery stalks or celery salt, sugar, salt and a pinch of paprika. Bring this to the boil and simmer for about twenty minutes then put the mixture through the Mouli – there should be about a pint of liquid pulp. Dissolve the gelatine in a little warm water and stir it into the tomato, adding a tablespoon of wine or tarragon vinegar. Pour into a mould and let it set firmly before turning out to serve.

This makes a decorative accompaniment to a main course, and is particularly good for those who are unable to eat tomato skins or pips. It can be made successfully with tinned tomatoes.

108 Potato Salad

Time taken: 30 mins

1 lb (450 g) potatoes
4 tablespoons oil
1 tablespoon vinegar
salt and pepper

1 small onion or shallot, chopped, if available
parsley, if available, chopped

Boil the potatoes in their skins if they are not too large, and when they are cool enough to handle skin them and cut them into slices

C

about a quarter of an inch (25 mm) thick. Make dressing from the oil, and vinegar, and a little salt and pepper. Put in the potatoes and mix them well, but carefully so that the slices do not break, and add the onion or shallot and parsley. Turn the potatoes again before serving, and if necessary, add more dressing, as they absorb a good deal.

Left-over boiled potatoes can be used for this if they are not too soft, but it is better made with freshly cooked potatoes, as if they are dressed while hot they absorb the flavour more.

109 Cucumber Salad

Time taken: preparation 10 mins; total time 1 hour

1 cucumber, peeled
salt
3 tablespoons oil, or 3 tablespoons sour cream

1 tablespoon vinegar
pepper
chives, if available, chopped

Slice the cucumber as thinly as possible. Put the slices on to a dish, sprinkle them with salt and leave them for a good hour so that the excess liquid runs from them. Drain the liquid off, and pour over the cucumber a dressing made from the oil and vinegar and a little pepper (no more salt is needed). As a change, sour cream can replace the oil in the dressing. Chives sprinkled on top make a good addition.

110 The Poet's Salad

This is the work of the Reverend Sydney Smith, a Canon of St Paul's in the last century. I give it here in the original then put into rather plainer language as written by Eliza Acton, in her *Modern Cookery for Private Families* (1848).

> Two large potatoes passed through kitchen sieve
> Unwonted softness to the salad give.
> Of mordant mustard, add a single spoon,
> Distrust the condiment which bites so soon;
> But deem it not, thou man of herbs, a fault,
> To add a double quantity of salt;
> Three times the spoon with oil of Lucca crown,

And once with vinegar, procured from town;
True flavour needs it, and your poet begs
The pounded yellow of two well-boiled eggs;
Let onion atoms lurk within the bowl,
And, scarce suspected, animate the whole;
And lastly, in the flavoured compound toss
A magic teaspoon of anchovy sauce;
Then, though green turtle fail, though venison's tough,
And ham and turkey are not boiled enough,
Serenely full, the epicure may say –
Fate cannot harm me, – I have dined today.

Two well boiled potatoes, passed through a sieve; a tea-spoonful of mustard; two teaspoonfuls of salt; one of essence of anchovy; about a quarter of a teaspoonful of very finely chopped onions, well-bruised into the mixture, three table-spoons of oil; one of vinegar; the yolks of two eggs, hard-boiled. Stir up the salad immediately before dinner, and stir it up thoroughly.

N.B. As this salad is the result of great experience and reflection, it is hoped young salad makers will not attempt to make any improvements upon it.

And a version by a Victorian poet, Mortimer Collins:

Take endive – like love it is bitter,
Take beet – for like love it is red:
Crisp leaf of the lettuce shall glitter,
And cress from the rivulet's bed:
Anchovies, foam-born, like the lady
Whose beauty has maddened this bard;
And olives, from groves that are shady;
And eggs – boil 'em hard.

Rice dishes

RICE IS VERY OBLIGING and has many advantages over potatoes as a vegetable. It doesn't need to be peeled, and can be cooked in the morning and reheated without harm in the evening. Drain it well after cooking, and when it is needed put it in a colander and pour boiling water through. This reheats it without further cooking or making it soggy. It looks good if it is pressed into a ring mould for a few moments after cooking, turned out and the centre filled with a chosen sauce. You can use the same sauces as for pasta, or make a pilaff using left-over meat or chicken, minced and mixed with onion and cooked rice, with a few sultanas.

111 Basic Ways of Boiling Rice

A. The easiest: Put one cup of rice into a saucepan, add two and a half cups of water or stock and a teaspoon of salt. Bring to the boil with the lid on the saucepan and when it is boiling stir once, turn down the heat, replace the saucepan lid and leave to cook undisturbed for about twenty minutes – the exact time varies with the different types of rice. Drain off any surplus liquid through the colander.

B. Have a large pan of salted water already boiling, pour in the rice slowly so that the water doesn't go off the boil, and cook rapidly in an uncovered pan. Drain well when cooked. Test for doneness by trying one or two grains.

C. The third basic way, the one for making a risotto, takes more time and attention. Italian rice is the best for this as the grains are larger and absorb liquid well. You need a good deal more liquid than for either of the previous methods. A pound (450 g) of rice will probably absorb three pints (1.8 litres) of water.

Melt half an ounce (15 g) of butter and stir the rice into this until it is well coated. Pour on a cupful of boiling stock (or water) and cook until the liquid is almost absorbed; then add more stock. Continue to add stock as needed until the rice is soft and the liquid absorbed, without letting the rice become dry.

112 *Almond Rice*   Time taken: 20 mins

8 oz (225 g) rice   2 oz (50 g) sultanas
2 oz (50 g) flaked almonds   lemon rind, grated

Cook the rice in plenty of salted water until tender, then drain it well. Toast the almond flakes until golden, and mix them into the rice together with the sultanas and a little grated lemon rind.

This goes well with any spicy dish, like curry or paprika chicken

113 *Spring Risotto*   Time taken: 30–40 mins

1 large onion, diced   1 tablespoon chopped parsley
2–3 carrots, diced   1 lb (450 g) rice
1 tooth garlic   3 pints (1.8 litres) approx.
2 oz (50 g) butter   stock, depending on the
4 oz (100 g) mushrooms,   rice
   sliced   3 oz (75 g) grated cheese

Sauté the onion and carrots with the garlic in the butter until the onion is transparent. Add the mushrooms to the vegetables with some chopped parsley, and cook them together for a few moments. Remove the garlic and add the rice, stirring it well until it is quite coated with the butter. Pour on a cupful of boiling stock. Cook gently until the stock is absorbed, then add another cupful and continue to cook like this, stirring the rice and adding the hot stock as it is absorbed. When the rice is cooked but still moist, check the seasoning and add an ounce (25 g) of grated cheese. Let the risotto settle a minute or so before serving with the remaining grated cheese.

This recipe uses only carrots, onions and mushrooms, but other vegetables such as peas, asparagus tips, and beans can be used.

114 Nasi Goreng

Time taken: 30 mins
(using cooked rice)

8 oz (225 g) rice
1 large onion, finely chopped
1 tablespoon oil
1 oz (25 g) butter
garlic
salt
½ teaspoon coriander

1 teaspoon paprika
4 oz (100 g) cooked ham or
 bacon, diced
6 oz (150 g) shrimps or
 prawns, fresh or tinned
3 eggs

Cook the rice (**No 111**). Cook the onion gently in a mixture of the butter and oil until yellow. Add a little garlic, salt, coriander, paprika, and the ham or bacon. Stir well, then add the cooked rice. Stir until all is well mixed and the rice browns a little. Add the prawns or shrimps if you have any (tinned ones will do perfectly well for this dish). Put the rice mixture into a serving dish and keep it warm while you make a flat omelette with three eggs. Cut this into strips and put it on top of the rice.

Cooked rice is used for this dish, so the rice can be boiled well ahead of time if necessary.

115 Kedgeree

Time taken: 30 mins

8 oz (225 g) rice
3 eggs
1 7½ oz (213 g) tin salmon,
 drained

1 oz (25 g) butter
salt and pepper
coriander or curry powder,
 if liked

Boil the rice and drain it well. Boil two of the eggs until hard, then shell them as soon as possible. Melt the butter in a saucepan, add the flaked salmon and the chopped hard-boiled egg and warm them through, stirring well. Add the cooked rice and mix it well with the fish and egg. Season with salt and pepper, and a little spice such as coriander or curry if you like. When all is well mixed, beat up the third egg and pour it over to moisten the rice. Serve hot.

This, I believe, is best made with smoked haddock, but tinned salmon or tuna fish, or kipper fillets can be used quite successfully.

116 Rice Cakes

Time taken: 20 mins

4 oz (100 g) cooked rice
1 egg
chopped parsley
salt and pepper

paprika
1 onion, very finely chopped
butter

Mix the well beaten egg into the rice which should preferably be warm or reheated, add the chopped parsley, salt, pepper and a little paprika. Cook the onion in a little butter until soft, then add it to the rice. Make small cakes of this mixture by putting spoonfuls on to a dish and flattening them with a fork. When ready to cook them, make some butter hot in a pan and fry the rice cakes, taking care when turning them as they break easily. They can be deep-fried if you prefer, in which case they will not need turning. Drain well before serving.

These little fried rice cakes make a change from potatoes.

117 Stuffed Cabbage or Vine Leaves

Time taken: preparation 30 mins; cooking 30 mins

12 cabbage leaves or 24 vine leaves
4 oz (400 g) rice
1 onion, finely chopped
1 tablespoon oil
8 oz (225 g) mushrooms (fresh, tinned or dried), chopped

or 8 oz (225 g) minced meat, cooked
salt and pepper
garlic
about ½ pint (3 dl) stock
egg and lemon sauce (No 8)

Blanch the cabbage or vine leaves in boiling water for a couple of minutes, then spread them out to cool. Boil the rice, and while it is cooking, fry the onion gently in the oil and mix with it either the mushrooms or the mince. Add the cooked and drained rice to this mixture and season well with salt, pepper and garlic. Spread the leaves out on to a board, put a little of the rice mixture in the centre of each, and roll them up neatly, tucking in the sides like a parcel. Place them side by side in a shallow pan, with the join underneath, packing them close together in the pan so that they will not unroll. Pour in enough stock to come halfway up the bundles, cover the pan and simmer gently for half an hour.

Dish them carefully so that they don't break or, if possible, cook them in a dish in which they can be served. Serve with egg and lemon sauce (**No 8**).

118 Rice Salad   Time taken: 20–30 mins

4 oz (100 g) rice
¼ pint (1.5 dl) (approx.)
  French dressing
3 tomatoes, skinned, seeded
  and chopped
1 stick celery, chopped
or 1 green pepper, seeded and
  chopped

4 oz (100 g) fresh peas,
  cooked, or tinned *petits
  pois*
2 oz (50 g) sultanas
½ cucumber, diced but not
  peeled
chopped parsley

Cook the rice (page 68) until it is soft, then drain well, and while it is still warm mix in about a quarter of a pint (1.5 dl) of French dressing – the exact amount depends on the rice, but it should absorb it well without becoming too oily. Let this cool before adding the tomatoes, celery or green pepper (which give crispness to the rice), peas, sultanas and cucumber. Mix all the ingredients well so that the red, white and green colours are blended and sprinkle with chopped parsley before serving very cold.

Allow an ounce (25 g) of rice per person if this is to be a side salad, two ounces (50 g) if it is to be a main dish.

119 Summer Curry Salad   Time taken: 30 mins

for the mayonnaise:
1 egg yolk
½ pint (3 dl) oil
1 teaspoon wine vinegar
1 level teaspoon curry
  powder
salt and pepper
parsley, finely chopped

4 oz (100 g) rice

4 eggs, hard-boiled
8 oz (200 g) prawns, shelled
  (or 6 oz (150 g) tinned
  prawns)
or flaked fish *or* chicken
anchovy essence
lettuce leaves
cucumber, sliced
4 tomatoes, skinned, seeded
  and halved

Make the mayonnaise (for method see **No 10**) and when it is mixed add the curry powder, salt and pepper and the finely chopped parsley. Boil the rice, drain it in a colander, run cold water through it, drain it again and put it into a ring mould until you are ready to use it. Remove the yolks from the hard-boiled eggs and mash them with a little mayonnaise and anchovy essence; then replace the yolks in the whites.

Turn out the rice mould on to a flat dish, and surround it with the lettuce leaves and cucumber slices. Fill the tomato shells with mayonnaise and arrange the tomatoes and eggs alternately around the rice ring. Mix the prawns or chicken with the rest of the mayonnaise and pile the mixture into the centre of the rice.

Pasta

120 *Macaroni Cheese*

Time taken: 40 mins

6 oz (175 g) macaroni
for the sauce:
1 oz (25 g) butter
1 oz (25 g) flour
1 pint (6 dl) milk
salt and pepper
1 tablespoon grated cheese

1 dessertspoon made mustard

1 onion, chopped
1 oz (25 g) butter
2 rashers bacon, diced
grated cheese

Cook the macaroni in boiling salted water until tender, but not mushy. Make the cheese sauce (**No 4**). Cook the onion until soft in the butter and add the bacon. Put a layer of macaroni into a pie dish, cover it with the onion and bacon and then the rest of the macaroni. Pour over the sauce, sprinkle with a little more grated cheese and heat through in the oven or brown under a hot grill.

121 *Curried Macaroni*

Time taken: 40 mins

Make this the same way, but use a curry cream sauce (**No 6**) instead of the cheese sauce and omit the bacon and onion layer.

122 Pasta (Spaghetti or Macaroni) with Sausage and Tomato

Time taken: 30 mins

2 onions, chopped
1 tablespoon oil
1 14 oz (397 g) tin tomatoes
¼ lb (100 g) mushrooms, fresh or dried and reconstituted

1 boiling sausage, sliced
salt and pepper
8 oz (225 g) spaghetti or macaroni

Fry the onions in the oil, and then add the tomatoes and mushrooms (if any). Cook together, then add the slices of boiling sausage and season with salt and pepper. Let this cook slowly until it thickens, and meanwhile boil the spaghetti or macaroni until tender. Drain the pasta well, put it into a large dish, pour the sauce over and serve hot.

Pasta can be served with Pesto (**No 17**), Spaghetti Sauce (**No 23**), or just with butter and grated cheese.

Spaghetti can be reheated by putting it into a colander over a pan of boiling water. Cover the colander and the steam will heat the pasta through. But if you intend to do this, slightly undercook the pasta in the first place, or it may get too soft.

123 Macaroni and Sausages

Time taken: 30 mins

6 oz (175 g) macaroni
6 rashers fat bacon, chopped
1 large onion, chopped
1 stalk celery, if any, chopped small
3 tablespoons water
2 tablespoons wine or herb vinegar

1 heaped teaspoon brown sugar
1 or 2 gherkins, finely chopped
salt and pepper
paprika
8 frankfurters, *or* slices of boiling sausage
parsley for garnish

Boil the macaroni in salted water until it is just cooked, then drain it well. Fry the bacon and onion until the fat runs from the bacon and the onion starts to soften. Add the celery if you have any. Mix together the water, vinegar and sugar, pour this mixture over the vegetables and bring to the boil. Stir in the cooked macaroni and the gherkins and season with salt and black pepper and a little paprika. Heat the frankfurters or slices of boiling sausage; turn the macaroni mixture on to a hot dish and put the sausages on top. Garnish with parsley.

Pasta is not usually thought of as an ingredient for a salad, but it makes a good change from rice or potato for a cold main dish. It is best to use the thicker pasta like short-cut macaroni or shells rather than spaghetti or noodles.

124 *Provençal Salad*   Time taken: 30 mins

8 oz (225 g) pasta shells or short-cut macaroni

for the dressing:
5 fl oz (1.5 dl) oil
salt and pepper
3 tablespoons vinegar
1 tooth garlic, crushed

3 eggs, hard-boiled
lettuce leaves
2 tomatoes, each cut into six pieces
6 anchovy fillets
capers or black olives for garnish

Cook the pasta shells or macaroni in two quarts of well-salted boiling water. Drain into a colander, pour cold water through and drain well. Mix the dressing and turn the drained pasta in it so that it is all well covered. Leave the pasta to get quite cold. Wash and shake dry some crisp lettuce leaves and put them on to a shallow dish. Make a ring of the pasta and in the middle of this put the hard-boiled eggs, cut in half lengthways and the tomatoes. Put an anchovy fillet on top of each egg half and pour over a little more of the dressing. You can use mayonnaise at this point if you prefer, though I find this a little too rich. Garnish with capers or black olives.

This is rather like a Salade Niçoise, and can be varied according to the ingredients at hand.

125 Waldorf Pasta Salad   Time taken: 30 mins

4 oz (100 g) pasta shells or
   short-cut macaroni
2 red apples, cored but not
   peeled
lemon juice
1 tin tuna fish, drained and
   flaked
1 stick celery, finely chopped
cooked peas, if any

1 tablespoon sultanas or
   raisins
either 2 fl oz (60 ml) French
   dressing
1 small carton plain yogurt
   or soured cream
or ¼ pint (1.5 dl) lemon
   mayonnaise
walnuts, if liked

Cook the pasta in well-salted boiling water until just tender, drain it, pour cold water through it and allow it to drain again thoroughly.

Dice the apples and dip the dice in lemon juice which helps to stop them turning brown. Turn the pasta, diced apples, tuna fish, celery and peas into a salad bowl, mix in some raisins or sultanas and toss the whole either in the French dressing which has been mixed with plain yogurt or soured cream or in a lemony mayonnaise. Add a few walnuts if liked.

Pastry dishes

FLANS OF ALL KINDS are very good for making a sustaining dish out of very little, and the fillings can be varied endlessly. Shortcrust pastry is easy to make and it can be made in advance, wrapped up in foil or greaseproof paper and kept in the refrigerator for a week; it can also be bought ready-made and stored in the refrigerator. In any case, shortcrust handles more easily and is lighter if it is allowed to rest in the refrigerator or cold larder for about half an hour between mixing and baking.

Most flans can be eaten hot or cold or just warm. If the filling is a soft one, or contains eggs, it is advisable to bake the flan case 'blind' before using it. This both prevents the filling from making the pastry soggy, and allows the pastry to 'set' by being cooked in a hotter oven than the eggs would take without curdling. To bake a flan case 'blind', cover the bottom of the flan with foil, scatter dried beans over it to stop the inside rising up, and bake for about fifteen minutes at 400°F/200°C/Regulo 6. The beans can be stored and used over and over again, but don't put them where they can be mistaken for fresh dried beans.

126 Granny Goward's Bacon Cake

Time taken: 1 hour
make in advance

8 oz (225 g) shortcrust pastry
8 oz (225 g) streaky bacon

6 eggs, lightly beaten
pepper

Preheat the oven to 400°F/200°C/Regulo 6. Divide the pastry into two, and line a seven-inch flan tin with one half, reserving the remainder for the top. Cover the pastry lining with the bacon rashers, then pour on to them half the eggs; add another layer of bacon, more egg and a final layer of bacon. Season with pepper only as the bacon will probably provide enough salt. Cover with the remaining pastry, seal the edges well, make two or three slits in the top, brush over with a little egg or milk and bake in the oven for about forty minutes.

127 Mustard Tart
Time taken: 1 hour

6 oz (175 g) shortcrust pastry
5–6 tomatoes
French mustard

4 oz (100 g) grated cheese
2 egg yolks
2 fl oz (58 ml) cream

Preheat the oven to 400°F/200°C/Regulo 6. Line an open flan case with the pastry and bake it blind for about fifteen minutes. Remove it from the oven and turn the oven down to 250°F/130°C/Regulo ½. Remove the skins and pips from the tomatoes and cut them in half. When the flan case is cool, cover the base with a good layer of French mustard, sprinkle over the grated cheese, and on this put the halved tomatoes, cut side down. Beat the egg yolks with the cream and pour this mixture over the tomatoes and cheese. Bake in the slow oven for about half an hour, or until set.

128 Onion and Cheese Flan
Time taken: 1 hour

6 oz (175 g) shortcrust pastry
3 medium onions, thinly sliced
1 oz (25 g) butter
8 oz (225 g) cottage cheese, plain or with chives

salt and pepper
2 eggs, beaten
grated Parmesan cheese, if liked
chopped chives or parsley

Preheat the oven to 400°F/200°C/Regulo 6, line a seven-inch (17.5 cm) flan tin with pastry and bake it blind for about fifteen minutes. Turn the oven down to 325°F/170°C/Regulo 3. Cook the onions in the butter until they are soft but not brown. Mix the cottage cheese with a little salt and pepper and the beaten eggs, adding a little grated Parmesan if you like a stronger cheese flavour. Put the softened onions on to the flan base, pour over the cheese mixture, sprinkle the top with chopped chives or parsley and bake in the oven for about half an hour or until firm.

129 Onion Tart — Time taken: 1 hour

shortcrust pastry made from
6 oz (175 g) flour, and 1½
oz (40 g) each butter and
lard
1½ lb (675 g) onions, finely
sliced

2 oz (50 g) butter
salt and pepper
cumin or coriander
5 fl oz (150 mls) sour cream
or plain yogurt
3 eggs, beaten

Preheat the oven to 400°F/200°C/Regulo 6 and meanwhile cook
the onions gently in the butter until they are soft and just beginning to darken – the easiest way is in a covered pan on a very low
heat. When they are soft, season them with salt, pepper and cumin
or coriander. Mix together the sour cream (or yogurt) and the
beaten eggs. Take the onions off the heat and allow them to cool
while you roll out the pastry to line a flan case. Put in the onions,
pour the egg mixture over them, and bake in the oven for about
half an hour. Serve warm.

This is different from the preceding recipe: it is the type found
in Alsace, and contains no cheese. The pastry should be made
from the mixture of butter and lard.

130 Salmon Flan — Time taken: 1 hour

6 oz (175 g) shortcrust pastry
1 8 oz (225 g) tin salmon (or
other fish, see below)
2 eggs
5 fluid oz (150 mls) cream or
top-of-the-milk

anchovy essence or
Worcestershire sauce
salt and pepper
anchovy fillets for garnish, if
liked

Preheat the oven to 400°F/200°C/Regulo 6, line an eight-inch flan
tin with the pastry and bake blind for fifteen minutes. Drain the
salmon liquid well, flake the flesh and spread it over the bottom
of the flan. Beat the eggs with the cream or top-of-the-milk,
season well with a little anchovy essence, or some Worcestershire
sauce, pepper and salt and pour this mixture over the fish. Put
back into the oven at 375°F/190°C/Regulo 5 for half an hour.
Garnish with the anchovy fillets if you like.

This can also be made with cooked smoked haddock if you

have some left over, or tinned kipper fillets, or prawns, or whatever there is.

131 *Quiche Lorraine*   Time taken: 1 hour

6 oz (175 g) shortcrust pastry   ¼ pint (1.5 dl) milk
1 oz (25 g) butter   salt and pepper
1 onion, finely chopped   2 eggs
2–3 streaky bacon rashers, cut   1 dessertspoon grated cheese
  in strips

Preheat the oven to 400°F/200°C/Regulo 6, line a flan case with the pastry and bake blind for fifteen minutes. Remove from the oven and leave it to cool while you cook the onion in the butter until soft. When the onion is nearly cooked, add the bacon and spread this mixture over the base of the flan. Mix the eggs with the milk, season and add the cheese. Pour this over the par-baked flan case and finish baking in a moderate oven (375°F/190°C/Regulo 5) for about half an hour, or until the filling is set.

There are very many versions of this dish, and everyone seems to have their favourite. This is one that I like, but some people prefer to leave out the onion, others the cheese.

132 *Tomato Croustade*   Time taken: 1 hour

6 oz (175 g) shortcrust pastry   *for the sauce:*
2 oz (50 g) butter   1 oz (25 g) butter
1 large onion, chopped   1 oz (25 g) flour
8 oz (225 g) tin tomatoes   ¼ pint (1.5 dl) milk
mixed herbs, dried   1 oz (25 g) grated cheese

Preheat the oven to 400°F/200°C/Regulo 6, line a flan tin with the pastry, and bake blind for fifteen minutes. Meanwhile soften the onion in the butter, and when it has cooked for a few minutes, add the tomatoes. Season well with salt, pepper, and a pinch of mixed herbs and cook gently, stirring from time to time, until the tomato and onion amalgamate and thicken. It is easiest to start the cooking with the pan covered, and then take the lid off so that the vegetables reduce, but without becoming too dry. Let them cook for about forty minutes, while you make a thick cheese sauce from the butter, flour, milk and grated cheese. Stir this well until it thickens then allow it to cool. Cover the base of the partly cooked flan case with the tomato and onion mixture, then spread or pipe in circles round the flan the thick cheese sauce. Put it back into the oven at 375°F/190°C/Regulo 5 until it is heated through and the cheese is beginning to turn golden (about 15 minutes).

133 Mushroom and Tuna Fish Flan

Time taken: 40 mins

for the pastry:
4 oz (100 g) mashed potato
4 oz (100 g) flour
2 oz (50 g) butter
for the filling:
1 oz (25 g) butter
1 onion, finely chopped

8 oz (225 g) mushrooms
  (fresh, tinned or dried),
  thinly sliced
1 tablespoon flour
½ pint (1.5 dl) milk
salt and pepper
8 oz (225 g) tin tuna fish

Preheat the oven to 400°F/200°C/Regulo 6. Mix the mashed potatoes with the flour and butter. Roll this out, line the flan case and bake blind for fifteen minutes. While it is cooking, make the filling. Cook the onion gently in the butter until it is soft, then add the mushrooms. Cook these for a few minutes, then sprinkle the flour over the vegetables, mix well and cook for a further minute. Gradually add the milk, stir until it is well absorbed, and season with salt and pepper. Flake the tuna fish with a fork and add it, stirring until everything is well mixed. Fill the par-baked flan case with the mixture and if there are any scraps of pastry left over, cut them into thin strips, twist them and lay them across the flan in a lattice pattern. Return the flan to the oven for a further fifteen minutes. Serve hot or warm.

This can also be made with 8 oz (225 g) of conventional short-crust pastry, but the potato pastry, which is very soft, makes a pleasant change.

134 Fitchet or Fidget Pie

Time taken: preparation
20 min; cooking 1½ hours

shortcrust pastry made from
8 oz (225 g) flour, 2 oz
(50 g) each lard and butter
1 lb (450 g) potatoes, peeled
1 large or 2 medium onions,
sliced

2 large cooking apples, or 3
dessert apples, peeled, cored
and sliced
½ lb (225 g) bacon, cut in
strips
salt and pepper
½ pint (3 dl) stock

Preheat the oven to 400°F/200°C/Regulo 6. Make the pastry and
leave it to rest. Meanwhile bring the potatoes to the boil in salted
water and cook them for five minutes, drain them, and when cool
enough cut them into fairly thick slices. Put a layer on the
bottom of a pie dish, cover them with a layer of onions, then
apples, then bacon, seasoning as you go. Repeat the layers until
the dish is full, finishing with a top layer of bacon. Pour in the
stock, cover the pie with the pastry, make a slit in the top of the
crust and brush over with milk or egg. Bake in the oven for half
an hour, then reduce the heat to 325°F/170°C/Regulo 3 for an
hour.

I don't know how this dish got its name, but it seems to have
originated in the Midlands. Anyway, it is good and tasty.

135 Basic Pizza Dough

Time taken: preparation
45 mins; cooking 15 mins

¼ oz (7.5 g) (2 teaspoons)
dried yeast
1 tablespoon warm water
8 oz (225 g) flour

1 teaspoon salt
1 tablespoon oil
water to mix

Dissolve the yeast thoroughly in the warm (not hot) water. Mix
the flour with the salt, add the oil, then pour in the yeast. Mix
well, adding two or three tablespoons of water to mix to a soft
but not wet dough. Knead this for a few minutes, then leave for
about half an hour. It will rise a little but not very much.

Heat the oven to 425°F/220°C/Regulo 7, divide the dough into
two and roll it out into two seven-inch (17.5 cm) circles. Put these

on to a greased plate or baking tray, prick the base well with a fork to prevent them rising in a bubble in the middle, and bake on the top shelf of the oven for about ten minutes, or until set and lightly browned at the edges. Take from the oven and cool until you are ready to put on the topping.

When the chosen topping is on, put the pizza back into the oven for ten minutes until it is well heated through and the cheese is melted. Serve hot.

The quantities given here make two seven-inch (17.5 cm) pizza bases, and should be enough for four big helpings or eight smaller ones according to appetite and what else there is to eat. I have found that if the base is par-baked before the filling is put on, there is less danger of the pizza becoming soggy and heavy as it too often is. It also means that the base can be made when convenient and the final cooking with the filling, which only takes five or ten minutes, done at the last minute.

136 Pizza Fillings

1. 1 lb (450 g) tomatoes, skinned and finely chopped
    or 1 tin tomatoes, drained well
    plenty of herbs
    anchovy fillets
    salami, thinly sliced
    grated cheese to cover

2. 1 lb (450 g) tomatoes, fresh or tinned
    1 onion, finely chopped and cooked in butter until soft
    bacon rashers, diced and cooked with the onion
    grated cheese to cover

3. 1 lb (450 g) tomatoes
    onions, sliced ⎫ cooked together
    mushrooms, sliced ⎭
    or tinned creamed onions with a tablespoon of tomato purée
        (no cooking needed)
    or dried mushrooms
    grated cheese to cover

4. 1 lb (450 g) tomatoes, beneath (in separate segments)
   (a) shrimps and mussels
   (b) anchovy fillets, washed in warm water, or soaked for 30 minutes in milk if they are too salt
   (c) soft cheese, diced
   (d) ham or salami, very finely sliced
   either grated cheese to cover, *or* a little oil with an egg broken on to the middle.

These are only suggestions. Only the tomatoes and cheese are essential. Otherwise use as much or as little as you like of what you have.

Egg dishes

OMELETTES CAN BE served folded or flat, and like flans or pancakes the fillings can be varied at will. Apart from the classic fillings, any bits of left-overs can be used to make a substantial meal when dressed up as an omelette. For a number of people it is perhaps better to make omelettes for one or two people at a time, rather than an enormous one, as these are easier to handle. As the method is the same in all cases, I give a basic recipe and suggestions for fillings.

137 Basic Omelette for One Person
Time taken: 10 mins

Beat two eggs (three if they are small) and season with salt. Heat a seven-inch (17.5 cm) pan and when it is hot add a little butter which should sizzle and turn brown quickly. Pour in the eggs to cover the pan, stir lightly with a fork, lifting the edges so that the raw egg runs underneath. When set at the bottom but still moist on top put the filling in, fold over and turn on to a hot dish.

138 Omelette Fillings

Onions: chopped finely and cooked until soft in butter; add to the omelette just before folding over.

Tomatoes: chopped and softened in butter.

Bacon: diced and cooked, with or without onion.

Mushrooms: sliced and cooked, or use tinned mushrooms in sauce.

Cheese: either mix a tablespoon of grated cheese into the egg mixture and proceed as for a plain omelette, or fold it into the omelette at the end.

Herbs: either put a good spoonful of fresh herbs into the mixture, or add it inside – parsley is particularly good. If using dried herbs, mix them into the egg as they are not moist enough for a filling.

139 Omelette Arnold Bennett   Time taken: 20 mins

6 oz (175 g) smoked haddock,   pepper
  cooked   butter
6 eggs   2 tablespoons cream
2 tablespoons grated cheese

Skin and flake the cooked haddock. Beat the eggs and add them to the fish, together with one tablespoon of the grated cheese. Season with pepper, but the fish is salty already so you probably will not need any more salt. Melt a little butter in an omelette pan, and when hot pour in the egg and fish mixture. Tip the pan a little so that the eggs cover the bottom and cook until the underneath is set.

Add the other spoonful of grated cheese, and the cream and put the omelette under a hot grill until the cheese is melted and the top of the omelette creamy but set. Serve the omelette flat, not folded.

140 Curry Omelette   Time taken: 15 mins

2 bacon rashers, diced   4 eggs
2 oz (50 g) cooked rice, either   2 teaspoons curry powder
  freshly cooked or left over   salt

Cook the bacon gently and add it to the rice. Mix the curry powder into the eggs. Make an omelette in the usual way and fill it with a tablespoon of the rice mixture before folding the omelette over and putting it on to a heated plate.

This is a good way of using up left-over cooked rice. The amount of filling should be enough for two people.

141 **Bauern Omelette**   Time taken: 25–30 mins

1 onion, sliced
1–2 oz (25–50 g) butter
3 potatoes, cooked and diced

3 rashers of bacon, diced
salt and pepper
4–6 eggs

Cook the onion gently in the butter until it softens but doesn't brown. Remove it from the pan and keep it warm, and in the same pan, adding more butter if necessary, lightly brown the potatoes. Add the bacon, season with pepper and very little salt, return the onions to the pan and mix well together until all are warmed through and cooked. Beat four or six eggs, according to size, pour them over the vegetables, and cook them without stirring until the bottom of the omelette has set but the top is still moist. Put the pan under a hot grill for a few moments to set the top – this is much safer and easier than trying to turn the omelette over – slide on to a hot dish, and serve.

142 **Spanish Omelette**   Time taken: 25–30 mins

1 onion, sliced
2 tomatoes, peeled, seeded
  and chopped
1 green pepper, if available

about ½ lb (225 g) peas, beans,
  or carrots
oil
1 tooth garlic, crushed
salt and pepper
4–6 eggs

Cook the vegetables in oil, or heat them through if you are using pre-cooked ones, and add a crushed tooth of garlic, salt and pepper. Beat the eggs, pour them over the vegetables in the pan and leave them until the eggs are set underneath, through the top will remain moist. Put the pan under a hot grill to set the top, slide on to a hot dish and serve.

This can be made with vegetables already cooked, or they can be cooked just before the eggs are added, as in the preceding recipe. The vegetables can be varied according to what you have, but usually include onions, tomatoes, peppers and peas or beans.

143 Piperade

Time taken: 20–30 mins

1 large onion, sliced
1 oz (25 g) butter
1 tablespoon oil
1 green pepper if available, cut
into strips, and deseeded

4 tomatoes, skinned and
chopped
1 tablespoon parsley, chopped
salt and pepper
4–6 eggs

Cook the onion gently in a mixture of butter and oil until soft. Add the pepper to the pan, then the tomatoes, together with the parsley and salt and pepper. When the vegetables are soft but not mushy, lower the heat under the pan. Beat four or six eggs, according to size; pour them over the vegetables and cook as for scrambled eggs, stirring so that the eggs and vegetables become well mixed. Serve hot as soon as possible.

This is made of similar ingredients to those in the Spanish omelette but the eggs are scrambled. Tinned red pepper can be used if you have no fresh green pepper, but the green gives a better contrast of colour.

144 Eggs Lyonnaise

Time taken: 30 mins

4 large onions, finely chopped
1½ oz (40 g) butter
6 eggs
1 tablespoon flour
¼ pint (1.5 dl) milk
1 bayleaf

salt and pepper
nutmeg
breadcrumbs
1 tablespoon parsley, chopped
bread }
oil } for garnishing

Stew the onions gently in the butter until they are soft and golden, but not in the least fried. Keep the pan covered while they are cooking to stop them drying up.

Meanwhile, boil the eggs for seven minutes so that the whites are set but the yolks not too hard. When they are boiled, plunge them into cold water straightaway and keep them there until you are ready to use them.

Add the flour to the onions, with the milk and bayleaf and season well with salt, pepper and a little nutmeg. Mix well, adding a little more liquid if it is too dry, and cook for another fifteen minutes. Peel the eggs very carefully – they are not as firm to handle as hard-boiled eggs – cut them lengthways into two or four pieces, put them into an earthenware dish and pour over them the onion mixture, removing the bayleaf first. Sprinkle with breadcrumbs and chopped parsley and brown quickly under a hot grill. Serve hot, with triangles of crisp fried bread arranged round the dish.

145 *Eggs in Nests*　　　　　Time taken: 15 mins

4 eggs
salt and pepper

2 oz (50 g) minced ham, *or* 4
　　slices ham, *or* 4 slices cheese
cheese sauce (**No 4**)

Preheat the oven to 350°F/180°C/Regulo 4. Separate the eggs, and keep each yolk whole – it is a good idea to prop up the half shell and keep the yolk in that for the moment. Beat the whites stiffly and fold in a little salt and pepper and the minced ham, if you are making the dish with this. Spread the whites on to rounds of toast and make a hollow in each, into which carefully put the yolks. Alternatively, put a slice of ham or cheese on to the toast underneath the whites. Put the egg nests on a baking sheet and bake in the oven for ten to fifteen minutes, or until the yolk is set and the meringue brown. Serve as soon as possible accompanied by a cheese sauce.

146 *Eggs in Potatoes (1)*　　　Time taken: 25 mins

1 lb (450 g) potatoes
1 onion, finely chopped
2 oz (50 g) butter
cream *or* top-of-the-milk

salt and pepper
mace
bacon or bread for serving
4 eggs

Boil the potatoes with the onion until soft, then mash them both smoothly with the butter and cream or milk, and season well with salt, pepper and mace. Make a bed of the potatoes in a thick layer on the serving dish, make four hollows in the mixture and keep it warm in the oven while you poach four eggs, which you then put into the hollows in the potatoes. Good just like this, but nicer if accompanied by rolls of crisp bacon or triangles of fried bread.

147 Eggs in Potatoes (2) Time taken: 40–50 mins

4 large potatoes 4 eggs
salt and pepper

Bake the potatoes in the oven until they are soft, then cut them
in half and remove most of the potato, leaving a skin shell. Mix
the potato pulp until smooth, season well and return to the shells,
making an indentation in the middle – extra pulp can be built up
round the hollow. Into each potato shell break an egg and return to
a moderate oven for about ten minutes, or until the eggs are set.

148 Curried Eggs (1) Time taken: 30 mins

6 eggs 1 onion, finely chopped
for the sauce: 1 tablespoon curry powder
2 oz (50 g) flour 6 oz (150 g) rice, boiled
2 oz (50 g) butter sultanas
1 pint (6 dl) milk *or* almond flakes
  chicken stock

Hard-boil the eggs, shell them as soon as possible and cut them
into slices. Make a thick curry sauce (**No 7**). When this has
cooked for a good twenty minutes put the slices of egg in a fireproof dish, cover with the sauce, heat thoroughly in the oven and
serve in a ring of boiled rice, to which a few sultanas and almond
flakes have been added.

149 Curried Eggs (2) Time taken: 25–30 mins

6 eggs parsley or other herbs, finely
1½ oz (40 g) butter   chopped
ham *or* mushrooms, if 1 egg, beaten
  available, chopped breadcrumbs or Matzo meal
1 pint (6 dl) curry sauce oil for frying
  (**No 7**) 6 oz (150 g) rice, boiled

Hard-boil the eggs, cut them in half lengthways and scoop out
the yolks. Mash them with butter, a little ham or some mushrooms, a spoonful of curry sauce and the herbs. Put this mixture
into the egg whites and mould them to look like the other half
of the egg, making twelve 'eggs' in all. Roll these in egg and

breadcrumbs, or Matzo meal, and fry them in hot oil until brown. Drain well on kitchen paper before serving with the rest of the curry sauce and plain boiled rice.

150 Egg Croquettes   Time taken: 30 mins

6 eggs

grated cheese or anchovy
    essence
salt and pepper

for the sauce:
1 oz (25 g) butter
1 oz (25 g) flour
¼ pint (1.5 dl) milk

1 beaten egg
breadcrumbs
oil for frying

Hard-boil the eggs, and chop them up finely. Make a well-seasoned thick white sauce with the butter, flour and milk. Grated cheese or a little anchovy essence can be added with advantage. Add the chopped eggs to this, mix well and allow to cool. Form into small cakes, dip in egg and breadcrumbs and fry until golden. Drain well and serve with tomato sauce (**No 25**) or onion sauce (**No 14**).

151 Scalloped Eggs   Time taken: 30 mins

6 eggs
1 small onion, finely chopped
1 oz (25 g) butter *or* 1
    tablespoon oil
3 or 4 rashers bacon, diced *or*
    cooked ham
4 oz (100 g) soft breadcrumbs

for the sauce:
½ oz (15 g) butter
½ oz (15 g) flour
½ pint (3 dl) milk
salt and pepper

breadcrumbs
grated cheese

Hard-boil the eggs, and slice them. Cook the onion until softened in the butter or oil, then add the bacon or ham. When the onion and bacon are nearly cooked put alternating layers of egg, breadcrumbs and the onion mixture into a dish. Pour over this the well-seasoned white sauce (**No 1**), sprinkle the top with breadcrumbs and a little grated cheese and brown in the oven.

Cheese sauce can be used instead of the plain white sauce if liked.

152 Eggy-Bread   Time taken: 10 mins

1 egg   6 slices bread
½ pint (3 dl) milk   butter and oil for frying
salt and pepper

Beat the egg with the milk and season with salt and pepper. Cut
the slices of bread into strips about an inch and a half (3.5 cm)
wide. Heat some butter or oil and butter in a frying-pan; dip the
bread pieces into the egg and milk mixture, then fry until brown
on both sides.

This is another good breakfast or tea dish, and very economical
as it makes one egg do for two or even three people. It can be
served with bacon or sausages.

153 Framed Eggs   Time taken: 10 mins

4 slices bread   4 eggs
butter and oil for frying

Trim the crust off the slices of bread, and cut a circle in the centre
of each, using a small pastry cutter. Heat the butter and oil in a
frying-pan, put in the bread and break an egg over each so that
the yolk falls into the hole. Fry for a moment or two, then turn
and fry the other side until the bread is golden and the egg
cooked.

These are good as they are for breakfast or children's tea, or
they can be smartened up by being served with a good tomato or
parsley sauce.

154 *Spicy Egg Mayonnaise*　Time taken: 20–30 mins

½ pint (3 dl) mayonnaise (No 10)
½ teaspoon paprika
1 or 2 gherkins, chopped
1 heaped teaspoon capers, chopped

1 large teaspoon Angostura bitters
tomato purée
garlic, if liked
6 eggs
parsley, watercress or radishes to garnish

Preheat the oven to 375°F/190°C/Regulo 5. Make the mayonnaise, and add to it the paprika, gherkins, capers, Angostura bitters and sufficient tomato purée to give the mixture a pleasant colour. Garlic can be added if you wish.

Butter an ovenproof dish well and break the eggs into it, very carefully so that the yolks remain whole. Cook in a *bain-marie* in the oven until the whites are set. It is a good idea to cover the dish with foil which helps to stop the egg whites becoming too hard. When the eggs are cold turn them out on to a dish, cover with the mayonnaise and garnish with whatever you have available.

Soufflés

These are not the obstacles they seem to be; the main thing is not to look at them in the oven until they have been cooking for twenty minutes and to serve them as soon as they are cooked, or they will lose their puffiness and begin to look rather sad. Don't make them unless you know exactly when you are going to be ready to eat them – if timing is uncertain use the same ingredients and make an omelette instead.

The basic mixture and method for all soufflés is the same.

155 *Basic Soufflé Method*　Time taken: preparation (can be done in advance) 20 mins; cooking 30 mins

1 oz (25 g) butter
1 oz (25 g) flour
¼ pint (1.5 dl) milk

3 eggs, separated
salt and pepper

Preheat the oven to 375°F/190°C/Regulo 5. Make a *roux* by melting the butter and stirring in the flour. Add the milk and cook until thick. Remove from the heat, add the beaten egg yolks and season. Beat the whites until stiff, fold them into the sauce mixture, pour into a prepared soufflé dish and bake in the oven for about half an hour. Don't look at it until it has cooked for this long, then see if the soufflé has risen and is fairly firm to the touch. If not, cook it a few more minutes. Serve as soon as possible.

156 Salmon Soufflé

1 oz (25 g) butter	3 eggs, separated
1 oz (25 g) flour	salt and pepper
¼ pint (1.5 dl) milk	1 7 oz (200 g) tin salmon

Make the basic sauce as above, keeping aside the egg whites. Drain the tinned salmon of all its liquid and mash the fish. Mix this into the soufflé sauce, then add the beaten white and carry on as before.

157 Cheese Soufflé: To the basic mixture add three ounces (75 g) of grated cheese, Parmesan if possible, and season with a little salt and pepper and a pinch of mustard.

158 Ham Soufflé: To the basic sauce add three ounces (75 g) of finely chopped cooked ham.

159 Tomato Soufflé: Make the basic sauce, but instead of using milk make it with tomato juice.

You can also use up small amounts of left-over chicken, fish or vegetable purée, such as spinach, but be careful that the filling is not too wet.

Pancakes and cheese dishes

LIKE OMELETTES AND SOUFFLÉS, once the basic pancake is made it can be filled with whatever you happen to have around, sweet or savoury. They can be filled with left-over meat or chicken, chopped or minced and mixed with a savoury sauce. They can be made well ahead, kept for up to a week in a refrigerator wrapped in foil, and warmed up when needed.

160 Basic Mixture for Savoury Pancakes

Time taken: preparation 10 mins; cooking 10 mins

4 oz (100 g) plain flour
salt
1 egg, beaten

½ pint (3 dl) milk and water, mixed
oil

Sieve the flour with a little salt, put it into a bowl and make a hollow in the middle. Pour the beaten egg into the hole and gradually add the milk and water mixture, beating all the time so that the batter gets smooth. Leave to stand for about an hour if possible. Beat again before using.

Heat a very little oil in a frying-pan so that it just covers the bottom of the pan. If there is too much, pour it off into a jug and keep it for the next pancake. When the oil is hot, but not smoking, pour in sufficient batter to cover the bottom of the pan and swirl the pan around a little so that the batter forms an even layer. When the underside of the pancake has set, shake the pan to loosen it, then either toss or turn it over to cook the other side. When it is cooked, turn it out of the pan, either on to a warm plate if you are going to use the pancakes at once, or to cool on a wire rack. If you want to keep them warm for immediate use, lay them on a warm plate put on top of a saucepan of hot water.

If you are going to use the pancakes later, when they are cool pile them on top of one another, wrap them in foil and store them in the refrigerator.

This quantity should make 8–10 seven-inch (17.5 cm) pancakes.

161 Bacon Pancakes

Time taken: 20 mins
(using prepared pancakes)

8–10 7-inch (17.5 cm)
  pancakes (above)
for the white sauce:
¼ oz (6 g) butter
¼ oz (6 g) flour
¼ pint (1.5 dl) milk
8 oz (225 g) cooked bacon or
  ham, finely chopped
pepper

2–3 gherkins, finely chopped
chopped parsley or dried
  herbs
1 tablespoon mustard
for the glaze:
1 oz (25 g) butter
2 tablespoons brown sugar
1 egg
1 dessertspoon mild mustard

Make the pancakes (above) and a white sauce (**No 1**). Mix the bacon or ham with the white sauce and the gherkins and sprinkle in some chopped parsley or dried herbs and the mustard. Put some of this filling on to the middle of the pancakes, roll them up and put them into a shallow fireproof dish. Mix the butter, brown sugar, egg and mustard together for the glaze, spoon it over the pancakes and brown them under a hot grill.

162 Onion Pancakes

Time taken: 25 mins
(using prepared pancakes)

8–10 7-inch (17.5 cm) pancakes
  (above)
2 large onions, finely chopped
2 oz (50g) butter
2–3 bacon rashers or ham
  slices, chopped

salt and pepper
1 tablespoon flour
2 tablespoons milk
3 tomatoes, skinned,
  de-seeded and chopped
1 tablespoon grated cheese

Make the pancakes (above). Stew the onions gently in an ounce (25g) of the butter until they are soft, then add the bacon or cooked ham and season well. Mix in the flour, moisten with the milk and cook until the onions are almost a purée, adding a little more liquid if

D

necessary. Put a line of filling down the centre of each pancake, roll them up and put them on to a shallow dish. Soften the tomatoes in the remaining butter, sprinkle on the grated cheese, put a little of this mixture on the top of the rolled-up pancakes and heat under the grill.

163 Here are some other suggestions for fillings

Mushrooms: finely sliced, cooked in butter and mixed with a thick white sauce.

Flaked fish: moistened with anchovy sauce and with a little extra sauce poured over the top.

Left-over meat or chicken: minced or chopped finely, mixed with curry sauce, and when cooked garnished along the top of the pancake with a little chutney.

164 Fraize or Froise   Time taken: 20–30 mins

This is an old English dish, and can be made with bacon cut into dice and fried, or with sausage meat, or flaked fish or apple (or with apple and bacon together). The filling varies with whatever is available, but the method of making the fraize is the same. It is really a pancake cooked with the filling mixed with the batter instead of used as a stuffing.

Make the pancake batter as usual. Fry the bacon or apple or whatever you are using, pour the batter over it in the pan and proceed as for pancakes, turning over to cook the top when the underside is done. They can then be rolled up like pancakes, or turned out on to a hot dish and served flat.

165 Toad in the Hole

Time taken: preparation
10 mins; cooking 45 mins

for the batter:

4 oz plain flour
salt
1 egg beaten
½ pint (3 dl) milk and water,
  mixed

1 lb (450 g) sausages, or a
  boiling sausage, sliced
dripping

Make a pancake batter and set it aside. Preheat the oven to
475°F/240°C/Regulo 9. Heat some dripping in a shallow dish and
put in the sausages, or sliced boiling sausage and heat through for
about five minutes. Pour the batter on top and cook in the hot
oven for about ten minutes, then reduce the heat to 425°F/220°C/
Regulo 7 for another half hour or until the batter is well risen and
brown.

166 Pancake Layer

Time taken: 30 mins
(using prepared pancakes)

8 pancakes (**No 160**)
2 large onions, sliced
1 oz (25 g) butter
2–3 tomatoes, skinned

¼ lb (100 g) mushrooms, if
  available, sliced
1 tin corned beef, diced
salt and pepper
Worcestershire sauce

Make eight pancakes (**No 160**) and keep them warm. Cook the
onions gently in the butter until they are almost soft, then add the
tomatoes and the mushrooms, if available. When the vegetables
are cooked and soft, add the corned beef. Season with salt, pepper
and a little Worcestershire sauce.

Put one pancake on a shallow dish, spread this with a tablespoon of the vegetables and meat; put another pancake on top
and spread it with the filling. Continue to make layers of the
pancakes and filling, keeping a little of the meat mixture for the
top. Put into the oven at 350°–375°F/180°–190°C/Regulo 4–5 to
get hot right through and serve, cutting it in wedges like a
cake.

Other meat or fish can be used instead of the corned beef, and
other vegetables can be added; this makes good use of left-overs.

167 Cheese Aigrettes

Time taken: preparation
(can be in advance) 15 mins;
cooking 10 mins

1 oz (25 g) butter
½ pint (3 dl) water
salt
cayenne

4 oz (100 g) flour
3 oz (75 g) grated cheese
2 eggs
oil for frying

Put the butter into a saucepan with the water and a seasoning of salt and cayenne. Bring the water to the boil, then add the flour, all in one go, and stir until it becomes a thick mass. Stir in the cheese, remove the saucepan from the heat and beat in the eggs, one at a time, waiting until the first is thoroughly mixed before adding the second. This becomes a thick springy paste, and should be left to cool until ready to finish the cooking. Heat some oil in a deep pan, drop in spoonfuls of the mixture and fry slowly until they are crisp and brown outside, but soft within. Drain well and serve hot. Tomato sauce is a good accompaniment, and so are crisply cooked bacon rolls.

168 Mint Cheesecake

Time taken: 40 mins

4 oz (100 g) butter
4 eggs, separated
4 oz (100 g) cheese, grated
2 tablespoons fresh mint,
  chopped

1 oz (25 g) self-raising flour
baking powder
¼ pint (1.5 dl) milk

Preheat the oven to 350°F/180°C/Regulo 4. Beat the butter with the egg yolks, then add the grated cheese and mint. When this is well mixed, add the self-raising flour to which a pinch of baking powder has been added, and a scant quarter pint of milk. Fold in the stiffly beaten egg whites, pour the mixture into a buttered soufflé dish and bake in the oven for about half an hour. Serve plain or with a tomato sauce.

This can also be made with raw minced meat substituted for the cheese.

169 Croque Monsieur

Time taken: 10 mins

4 slices bread
butter
2 slices ham

2 slices cheese
oil for frying

Cut two slices of bread for each person. Spread them thinly with butter on one side, and on this put a slice of ham and a slice of cheese. Make a sandwich with the other piece of bread and press the two pieces together. When all the sandwiches are ready, heat a frying-pan with two tablespoons of butter and a little oil. When this is hot, put in the sandwiches and fry them quickly until brown on each side. The cheese should just have time to melt without the bread browning too much.

These quantities are for two people. Substitute a little minced chicken for the ham and you have Croque Madame.

170 Gnocchi

Time taken: preparation
(can be in advance) 15 mins;
cooking 10 mins

2 oz (50 g) semolina
½ pint (3 dl) milk
½ teaspoon made mustard
salt and pepper
3 oz (75 g) cheese, grated

either:
egg and breadcrumbs for
   coating
tomato sauce (**No 25**)
or:
butter

Cook the semolina in the milk until it thickens as it boils. Stir well so that the mixture is smooth. Season with the mustard, salt and pepper and two ounces (50 g) of the grated cheese. When the mixture is cooked, pour it on to a dish in a layer about half an inch thick and let it cool. When it is quite cold, cut it into inch squares. Then *either:* dip them into egg and breadcrumbs, fry them and serve them with the remaining grated cheese and a tomato sauce, *or:* butter a fireproof dish, arrange the gnocchi slightly overlapping in the dish, and sprinkle them with the remaining grated cheese and little dabs of butter. Then put them into a hot oven, or under the grill, to heat and colour. The cooking can all be done well ahead of the meal, and the heating-up at the last minute.

171 *Welsh Cheese Pudding*   Time taken: 1 hour

4 slices bread	mustard
butter	nutmeg
8 oz (225 g) grated cheese	1 pint (6 dl) milk
salt and pepper	1 egg

Preheat the oven to 350°F/180°C/Regulo 4. Toast the bread slices on one side only, and butter the untoasted side. Put two of the slices, toast side down, on to a greased fireproof dish. On this, put four ounces (100 g) of the grated cheese and season with a little salt, pepper, mustard and nutmeg. Put the other pieces of bread again toast side down, on top and cover with the remaining cheese. Bring the milk to the boil, season and mix in the well-beaten egg. Pour this mixture over the bread and cheese and leave for about half an hour until it is absorbed. Bake in the oven for half an hour when it should be puffed up and golden. Serve hot.

This makes two good or four small portions.

172 *Cheese Pudding*   Time taken: 40 mins

1 pint (6 dl) milk	1 oz (25 g) butter
4 oz (100 g) soft breadcrumbs	2 eggs, separated
3 oz (75 g) grated cheese	salt and pepper

Preheat the oven to 375°F/190°C/Regulo 5. Bring the milk to the boil, pour it over the breadcrumbs and let them soak up the milk. Add the cheese, butter and the beaten egg yolks. Season with salt and pepper, fold in the well-beaten egg whites, pour the whole into a well-buttered dish and bake in the oven for about half an hour, or until well risen and set.

173 *Cheese and Potato Pie*   Time taken: 1⅓–1½ hours

1½ lb (675 g) potatoes, peeled and cut into thin rounds	mace
	salt and pepper
2 onions, finely chopped	½ pint (3 dl) stock
butter	2 eggs
6–8 oz (175–225 g) cheese, grated	¼ pint (1.5 dl) cream

Preheat the oven to 375°F/190°C/Regulo 5. Into a buttered casserole put a bed of sliced potato, then a layer of onion and a layer of grated cheese; season with mace, salt and pepper. Pour over a quarter of a pint (1.5 dl) of the stock and repeat the layers until the dish is two-thirds full. Beat the eggs with the cream and pour this over the pie. Put into the oven for about an hour or until cooked through and brown. Serve as it is from the dish.

174 *Welsh Rabbit*   Time taken: 15 mins

4 tablespoons milk or beer
8 oz (225 g) cheese, grated
Worcestershire sauce
mustard

pepper
1 egg yolk
4 slices toast

Warm the milk (or beer) in a saucepan, then stir in the grated cheese and season with Worcestershire sauce, a little mustard and pepper. Stir until the cheese melts, then beat in an egg yolk and warm through slowly until the mixture thickens. Pour the cheese mixture over the slices of toast and brown under a hot grill.

175 *Buck Rabbit*

Make the mixture as above, but serve with a poached egg on top.

176 *Mother's Supper*
(another Welsh dish)   Time taken: 40–45 mins

8 rashers bacon, or slices of
   ham
2 onions, finely chopped

4 oz (100 g) cheese, grated
salt and pepper
mustard powder

Preheat the oven to 400°F/200°C/Regulo 6. Put four of the bacon rashers or ham slices on to the bottom of a shallow fireproof dish. Cover them with the onions and cheese. Season with salt, pepper and a little dry mustard and top this with the other four rashers or slices. Cook in the oven for half an hour until the bacon is crisp on top. Serve with baked potatoes.

Meat and fish dishes

THE SMALL VACUUM-packed bacon joints are very useful to keep in store, and keep well. Also for many dishes that do not need tidy pieces of bacon, the trimmings, often rather fat, from the bacon slicer can be bought quite cheaply, and serve a good purpose both for flavour and substance instead of the more expensive joints.

The next seven recipes are written with this in mind, but of course the same dishes can be made with the bigger cuts.

177 Bacon Pizza

Time taken: preparation 15 mins; cooking 20 mins

for the base:
4 oz (100 g) self-raising flour
1 tablespoon melted butter
salt
water to mix
1½ oz (40 g) butter
1 tablespoon oil

for the top:
1 onion, finely chopped
1 oz (25 g) butter
1 small tin tomatoes, chopped
pepper
marjoram or thyme
6 rashers bacon
2 oz (50 g) cheese, sliced or
   coarsely grated

Mix the flour, salt and melted butter with sufficient water to make a soft dough. Roll out to make a round of about seven inches (17.5 cm) diameter. Heat the butter and oil in a frying-pan, put in the dough round and cook over a moderate heat for about five minutes.

Meanwhile, cook the onion in the butter, add the chopped tomatoes, season with pepper and a sprinkling of marjoram or thyme and cook until the liquid is reduced and the vegetables softened into a thickish purée. Fry or grill the bacon rashers on one side only. Turn the dough round over carefully, and spread it with the tomato and onion mixture, arrange the bacon, cooked side downwards, on top and sprinkle with the cheese. Put the pizza under a preheated grill to finish cooking, and to melt the cheese.

Real pizza should be made with a bread dough using yeast, but this is quick to make as it is made with an ordinary pastry dough. The cheese should be a mild Cheddar or any cheese that melts quickly.

178 Bacon Stew with Beans

Time taken: preparation overnight soaking for beans; cooking 1½–2 hours

2 oz (50 g) butter beans, soaked overnight
1½ lb (675 g) bacon joint
2 onions or leeks, sliced
1½ oz (40 g) butter

2 oz (50 g) plain flour
1 pint (6 dl) stock
2–3 carrots, sliced
pepper

Cut the bacon joint into inch squares, put them into cold water, bring them slowly to the boil and simmer for five minutes; then drain well.

Melt the butter in the saucepan and cook the onions or leeks gently until they begin to soften. Stir in the flour, add the stock and bring to the boil. Add the carrots, the drained butter beans and the bacon, season with pepper only, and cook in a covered pan for an hour and a half.

If you have no time to soak the butter beans, use a tin instead, and add them at the very end to heat through.

179 Bacon Balls

Time taken: 30 mins

1½ lb (675 g) bacon joint
2 onions
2 eggs
1½ oz (40 g) flour

3 tablespoons milk
pepper
allspice
3 oz (75 g) butter for frying

Mince the bacon joint with the onions – unless you have a very fine mincer, put it through twice. Mix with the flour, eggs and milk. Season with a little pepper and allspice – not salt as the bacon will probably be salty enough. Form into small balls and fry in the butter until cooked through.

180 Bacon Loaf

Time taken: preparation
20 mins; cooking 1 hour

Use the same mixture as for the bacon balls, but substitute one and a half ounces (40 g) of soft breadcrumbs for one of the eggs, and bake in a loaf tin for an hour in a moderate oven. Serve cold, cut into slices.

181 Bacon Roll

Time taken: preparation
25 mins; cooking 1–1½ hours

8 oz (225 g) bacon, finely
  chopped
1 large onion, diced
¼ lb (100 g) mushrooms, if
  available

6 oz (175 g) self-raising flour
3 oz (75 g) suet
salt
chopped parsley

Fry the bacon and onion together until softened, adding the mushrooms if you have any. When they are cooked, remove them from the fire and allow them to cool while you make a suet pastry with the flour, suet, a little salt and sufficient cold water to mix. Preheat the oven to 375°F/190°C/Regulo 5. Roll out the pastry into an oblong, spread it with the bacon–onion mixture to within about half an inch of the sides, and sprinkle with chopped parsley. Dampen the edges of the pastry, roll it up tightly and place it on a greased baking sheet. Cook it in the oven for an hour and serve it hot, with tomato sauce (**No 25**).

This can also be steamed: wrap the roll in foil and steam it for an hour and a half.

182 Bacon Casserole

Time taken: preparation
15 mins; cooking 1½ hours

1½ lb (675 g) bacon joint,
cut into cubes
1 onion, chopped
½ lb (225 g) tomatoes,
skinned and chopped, *or* 1
tin tomatoes

3–4 potatoes
pepper
mixed dried herbs
½ pint (3 dl) stock (made
from a stock cube, if
necessary)

Preheat the oven to 350°F/180°C/Regulo 4. Put the bacon cubes
into a casserole with the onion, tomatoes and potatoes. Season
with pepper and a sprinkling of herbs. Pour the stock over the
mixture, cover the pan and put into the oven for an hour and a
half.

183 Bacon Croquettes

Time taken: 20 mins

1 lb (450 g) cooked bacon or
ham, minced
1 lb (450 g) mashed potatoes
1 teaspoon French mustard

pepper
egg and breadcrumbs for
coating
fat for frying

Mix the minced bacon or ham with the mashed potatoes, add a
good teaspoon of French mustard, and season with pepper. Form
into small cakes, roll in egg and breadcrumbs and fry in hot fat
until golden.

184 Corned Beef Hash

Time taken: 20 mins

1 lb (450 g) cooked potatoes
1 tin corned beef
1 large onion, sliced

1 tablespoon dripping
1 tablespoon milk or water

Cut the potatoes into chunks and dice the corned beef. Cook the
onion gently in the dripping in a frying-pan, and when it is soft,
add the potato and corned beef, and moisten with a tablespoon of
milk or water. Cook on a very low heat until the bottom is brown,
then turn the mixture over and brown the other side. Serve very
hot.

185 Corned Beef Pie   Time taken: 30 mins

1 tin corned beef
1 onion, finely chopped
dripping
½ pint (3 dl) brown sauce (**No 2**)
  or tomato sauce (**No 25**)

Worcestershire sauce
1 lb (450 g) cooked potatoes
1 oz (25 g) butter

Soften the onion in a little dripping, add the roughly mashed corned beef and cover with the brown or tomato sauce, adding a good dash of Worcestershire sauce. Mash the potatoes and stir in the butter, lay them over the sauce and heat through in a hot oven, or brown under the grill.

186 Dublin Coddle   Time taken: preparation
                                           15 mins; cooking 1 hour

½ lb (225 g) streaky or
  knuckle bacon, cut into
  one-inch cubes
3 onions, thinly sliced
1½ lb (675 g) potatoes
1 lb (450 g) pork sausages, *or*
  smoked boiling sausage *or*
  frankfurters (tinned if
  necessary)

1 bunch parsley
salt and pepper
cornflour, if wanted
chopped parsley

Blanch the bacon for a few moments in water and drain it well. Put it into a large casserole with the onions and the potatoes, cut into halves if they are very big. Add the sausages and the bunch of parsley. Season with salt and pepper, and add sufficient water just to cover the ingredients. Cover the casserole and simmer gently for about an hour or until all the ingredients are cooked, removing the lid for the last fifteen minutes of cooking. The potatoes should be very soft and thicken the liquid sufficiently themselves, but if you like, thicken it some more with a little cornflour. Remove the bunch of parsley and serve sprinkled with fresh parsley.

187 Sausage and Mixed Vegetables
Time taken: 30 mins

1 small cabbage or ½ lb (225 g) sprouts
1 green pepper, if available
2 carrots
1 onion

1 or 2 celery stalks
2 oz (50 g) butter
salt and pepper
1 smoked boiling sausage
lemon juice

Prepare the vegetables and keep them in warm water until ready for cooking, then slice them and cook them gently in the butter until they are cooked but still a little firm. Season with salt and pepper. Cut the sausage into thick slices, and add them to the vegetables, together with a little lemon juice. Finish cooking the vegetables with the sausage and serve hot.

The six following dishes are all made from previously cooked meat, either minced or sliced, and are particularly good for making use of 'left-over' meat or poultry. You can also mince left-over meat or chicken, form it into rissoles, fry them until brown on both sides, and serve them with a tomato sauce (No 25) or onion sauce (No 14). Or mince the meat, mix it with a finely chopped onion, season well, cover with a lid of mashed potato and bake as cottage pie (or use an egg beaten up with a carton of yogurt to make a simple moussaka).

188 Baked Mince
Time taken: 30 mins

cooked meat, minced
1 onion
butter

Worcestershire sauce
tomato purée
soft breadcrumbs

Cook an onion in butter until softened, mix in some minced cooked meat, and moisten with a little Worcestershire sauce and tomato purée. Put the mixture into a pie dish and cover it with a layer of fresh breadcrumbs about half an inch thick. Pour an ounce or more of melted butter over the crumbs and bake in a moderate oven until the meat is heated through and the top is crisp and brown.

189 Durham Cutlets   Time taken: 20–30 mins

¼ lb (100 g) cooked meat,
  minced
1 oz (25 g) butter
1 oz (25 g) flour
¼ pint (1.5 dl) stock

3–4 tablespoons soft
  breadcrumbs
salt and pepper
Worcestershire sauce
egg and dried breadcrumbs
oil for frying

Melt the butter and mix the flour into it, then add the stock and
cook until thick. Mix the minced meat with the fresh breadcrumbs and season well with salt, pepper and Worcestershire
sauce. Cool, then form into a cutlet shape, dip in beaten egg and
then dried breadcrumbs and fry until brown in hot oil.

190 Kromeskies   Time taken: 20–30 mins

4 oz (100 g) cooked chicken,
  or other meat, minced
¼ pint (1.5 dl) thick white or
  brown sauce (Nos 1 & 2)

bacon rashers
frying batter (No 160)
fat for frying

Make the white or brown sauce and mix the chicken into it. Let
it cool, then form it into sausages. Wrap each one in a rasher of
bacon, dip into frying batter and fry until golden in hot fat.

These are usually made with left-over chicken, but any cooked
meat can be used the same way.

191 Norman Hash   Time taken: 25 mins

1 lb (450 g) onions
1 oz (25 g) butter
1 tablespoon flour
¼ pint (1.5 dl) red wine
¼ pint (1.5 dl) stock

salt and pepper
lemon juice (if available)
cooked beef or other meat,
  cut into neat slices

Cook the onions in butter until they are lightly browned, then stir
in the flour. Mix well and let the flour cook for a minute or two,
then pour in the red wine and stock. Season with salt, pepper and
lemon juice if you have any, and cook until the onions are quite
soft. Put the slices of meat into the onion sauce until they are quite
heated through and serve as soon as possible.

This is best made with small pickling onions, but two or three large onions sliced serve as well.

192 *Meat Cake*

Time taken: preparation
15 mins; cooking 30 mins

1 lb (450 g) cooked meat or
  chicken, minced
2 eggs, hard-boiled
4 oz (100 g) soft breadcrumbs
1 onion, finely chopped

chopped parsley
salt and pepper
1 egg
stock, or tomato purée diluted
  with water

Preheat the oven to 350°F/180°C/Regulo 4. Cut the hard-boiled eggs in slices and put them on the bottom of a buttered pie dish. Mix the minced meat or chicken with the breadcrumbs, the onion, the parsley, salt, pepper and the well-beaten egg. Moisten with a little stock, or tomato purée diluted with water. Mix well, put into the pie dish and bake in the oven for half an hour. Turn out so that the eggs are on top, and serve with a brown sauce (**No 2**) or tomato sauce (**No 25**).

193 *Bobbity*

Time taken: preparation
15 mins; cooking 30 mins

1 lb (450 g) cooked meat,
  minced
2 oz (50 g) butter
2 large onions, finely chopped
1 tooth garlic, crushed

1 dessertspoon curry powder
1 slice bread
1 dessertspoon chutney
2 eggs
2–3 tablespoons stock

Preheat the oven to 350°F/180°C/Regulo 4. Melt the butter in a pan, and cook the onions and garlic in this until soft. Add the curry powder and continue to cook for a few more minutes, then add the minced meat. Remove the crust from the slice of bread, soak it in water, squeeze it out, and mash it into the mixture. Add a spoonful of chutney, beat up one of the eggs with the stock and mix it into the meat. Season if necessary and put the whole into a well-buttered pie dish. Beat up the other egg and pour it over. Cook in the oven for half an hour.

This is a sort of minced curry.

194 Salmon Fishcakes

Time taken: 30 mins

1 8 oz (225 g) tin salmon
½ lb (225 g) potatoes, well
    mashed
anchovy essence, if wanted

egg and breadcrumbs, *or*
    flour
oil for frying

Drain the salmon of any liquid and mix it with the mashed potatoes; moisten if necessary with a little anchovy essence. Form into cakes, roll in egg and breadcrumbs, or flour, and fry until brown on all sides.

Tinned salmon makes excellent fishcakes or pies.

195 Salmon Pudding

Time taken: preparation
15 mins; cooking 30–45 mins

1 8 oz (225 g) tin salmon
3 oz (75 g) white breadcrumbs
1 teaspoon anchovy essence
2 tablespoons cream

2 eggs
salt and pepper
anchovy sauce (**No 3**) if liked

Preheat the oven to 350°F/180°C/Regulo 4. Mash the well-drained salmon and mix it lightly but thoroughly with the breadcrumbs, anchovy essence, cream and the well-beaten eggs. Season with salt and pepper. Put the mixture into a well-buttered soufflé dish and bake in the oven for half to three-quarters of an hour, or until it is set. Serve as it is, or accompanied with an anchovy sauce (**No 3**).

This pudding is more solid than a soufflé, and less sensitive to exact timing.

196 Fish Scallops

Mix left-over cooked fish with a thick white sauce, and if there is only a very little to be made to stretch a long way, add two finely chopped hard-boiled eggs. Put the mixture into scallop shells or a pie dish, cover with a thick layer of breadcrumbs, pour over melted butter and put into a hot oven for the dish to heat through and for the top to crisp and brown.

197 Fishcakes

The same mixture can be made into small cakes, rolled in flour, or egg and breadcrumbs, and fried. This makes nicer and lighter cakes than fish mixed with mashed potato (though if you have some left-over potato that is one way of using it up).

198 Salad Niçoise   Time taken: 20–30 mins

4 eggs, hard-boiled
1 7 oz (200 g) tin tuna fish,
  drained and flaked
½ cucumber, sliced
½ lb (225 g) cooked peas or
  beans

4 tomatoes, skinned and sliced
French dressing
black olives
anchovy fillets
8 oz (225 g) rice (see below)

Cut the hard-boiled eggs into halves or quarters, and mix them into a bowl with the tuna fish, cucumber and peas or beans. Add the tomatoes on top, pour the French dressing on to the salad, and garnish with black olives and anchovy fillets.

If you wish to make this more substantial, make a bed of boiled rice, dressed with French dressing while still warm, in the bottom of the bowl and put the Salad Niçoise on top.

Puddings

THE PUDDING COURSE presents less difficulty than any other in terms of store-cupboard ingredients: eggs, sugar, milk and fruit (fresh, bottled or dried) can be turned into all sorts of dishes, plain or fancy. Some of these are very simple, some rather more elaborate, but it often happens that a very plain meal can be elevated by a delicious last course, as that seems to be the one that people remember most.

You can keep the basis for one instant last course in the store-cupboard. Put dried apricots or prunes into a screw-top jar, and top them up with brandy or sweet wine, allowing space for the fruit to swell as it absorbs the liquor. You can eat them either as they are, or use the fruit in a fool and drink the liquid as a liqueur.

Any left-over cooked fruit, such as rhubarb, apricots, goose-berries or blackberries can be made into a kind of fool by puréeing it and then mixing it with plain yogurt, bought or home-made (No 249). Fruit like apple, without a marked flavour, is better used as the filling for a turnover or crumble.

Custards make the bases of several of these puddings, using only egg yolks. The whites can be used in other dishes or for meringues; they can be kept in a covered dish in the refrigerator for several days.

Here are two basic custard recipes, one for a baked custard which can be made richer by using the yolks only or lighter by using the whole egg. The 'boiled' custard is what custard ought to be when used for sauce, or for trifle or for anything else, and is very different from the custard-powder that unfortunately we accept now as the real thing. Many custards are baked in a *bain-marie*: this means simply that the custard dish is put into a tin or container with water to come halfway up the dish. It helps to prevent the custard cooking too fast and possibly curdling.

199 *Baked Custard*

Time taken: 30–40 mins

1 pint (6 dl) milk
4 egg yolks *or* 2 whole eggs

2 oz (50 g) sugar, preferably
vanilla

Preheat the oven to 325°F/170°C/Regulo 3. Bring the milk to boiling point, and beat the yolks or whole eggs with the vanilla sugar until thick. Pour the hot milk slowly on to them, stirring as you do so, until it is well mixed. Put the mixture into a shallow ovenproof dish or four small ramekins and cook in a *bain-marie* for about half an hour or until an inserted skewer comes out clean.

This custard can be flavoured with chocolate instead of vanilla if preferred, in which case use plain sugar.

200 *Custard*

Time taken: 15–20 mins

3 oz (75 g) sugar, preferably
vanilla

3 egg yolks, *or* 2 whole eggs
1 pint (6 dl) milk

Mix the sugar with the egg yolks or whole eggs, and beat until they are thick and creamy. Bring the milk to boiling point, pour a little into the eggs and sugar to mix, then return the whole to the saucepan. Cook slowly, stirring all the time, until the mixture thickens enough to coat the back of the spoon, but do not let it boil. When it is thick, pour it into a shallow dish to cool. Cook the custard in the top of a double boiler, or in a bowl over boiling water if you fear that it will boil and curdle. It takes longer that way but is safer. If you want the custard thicker use less milk – or more eggs.

201 *Crème Caramel*

Time taken: preparation
15 mins; cooking 30–45 mins

for the caramel:
4 oz (100 g) sugar
4 tablespoons water

for the custard:
3 eggs
1 tablespoon sugar
salt
1 pint (6 dl) milk

First make the caramel: boil the sugar with the water until it turns a warm brown. Pour it into a greased soufflé dish or individual ramekins, so that it completely coats the bottom of the mould.

Preheat the oven to 325°F/170°C/Regulo 3. Beat the eggs with the sugar and a pinch of salt. Heat the milk to simmering point, then pour it on to the eggs, stirring well. Pour the mixture into the dish or ramekins, put into a *bain-marie* with water coming halfway up the sides, and bake for about forty-five minutes, or until a knife inserted into the crème comes out clean. Leave it to get quite cold before turning it out and serving.

202 *Caramel Custard*

Time taken: preparation 15 mins; cooking 30–40 mins

2 oz (50 g) sugar
2 tablespoons water

1 pint (6 dl) milk
3 eggs, beaten

Preheat the oven to 325°F/170°C/Regulo 3. Boil the sugar and water together until golden brown. Add the hot milk to this and stir until the caramel is dissolved, pour this mixture on to the beaten eggs and bake in the oven in a *bain-marie* for about forty minutes. Test with a knife to see if the custard is set.

This is not the same thing as the preceding recipe as the caramel is mixed into the custard, and it makes a rich but not over-sweet dish.

203 *Crème Bacchique*

Time taken: preparation 10 mins; cooking 30–40 mins

½ pint (3 dl) sweet white wine
2 oz (50 g) sugar
2 tablespoons water

1 pint (6 dl) milk
3 egg yolks, beaten

Preheat the oven to 325°F/170°C/Regulo 3. Bring the wine to simmering point. Beat the egg yolks and sugar together until thick. Stir the hot wine slowly into the eggs, pour into individual ramekins and bake in a *bain-marie* in the oven for about forty minutes or until set.

204 Liqueur Custard
Time taken: 20 mins

½ pint (3 dl) milk
salt
2 tablespoons sugar

3 tablespoons liqueur
4 egg yolks
2 tablespoons cream

Mix the hot milk with a pinch of salt, the sugar and the liqueur. Beat the egg yolks with the cream and pour the milk mixture on to the eggs, stirring well. Return the whole to the saucepan and thicken over a gentle heat; do not let the custard boil. Serve cold.

This is a good way of using up any remains of liqueurs or miniature bottles.

205 Crème Brûlée
Time taken: preparation
15 mins; cooking 40–45 mins

3 egg yolks
3 oz (75 g) caster sugar

½ pint (3 dl), single cream (or
half cream, half milk)
granulated sugar

Preheat the oven to 300°F/150°C/Regulo 2. Mix the caster sugar with the egg yolks. Heat the cream nearly to boiling point, then whisk it into the egg mixture. Return the mixture to the saucepan and continue to stir until it thickens. Pour it into a fireproof dish, or better still four individual ramekins, and bake in the oven for about three-quarters of an hour.

Remove the dish or dishes from the oven and let them cool. When they are cold, sprinkle the top with an even layer of sugar so that the custard is quite covered, and put under a very hot grill so that the sugar melts and turns brown. Leave them to get quite cold so that the sugar forms a smooth crisp top but do not put them into the refrigerator once the sugar is caramelised as it may get soft and lose the delicious contrasting texture of crisp sugar and soft custard.

206 Zabaglione Gritti   Time taken: 15 mins

3 egg yolks
1½ oz (40 g) caster sugar
3 tablespoons marsala *or*
  full-bodied sherry

1 teaspoon powdered gelatine,
  if needed

Put the egg yolks into a bowl or the top of a double boiler with
the sugar and the marsala or sherry. (Dissolve the gelatine in a
little warm water and add this to the egg mixture.) Put the bowl
over a pan of hot water and beat steadily until the mixture thickens,
using a bowl that allows for the mixture to treble in size. When it
is thick, remove it from the heat and continue to beat it until
it is cool. Pour it into glasses and leave it to get quite cold.

If you are going to eat it straight away, there is no need to use
the gelatine, but it is sometimes tricky to get the right consistency
so that the mixture doesn't separate if kept waiting. It therefore
helps to stabilise it by using a little gelatine.

207 Queen's Pudding   Time taken: preparation
15 mins; cooking 45 mins

1 pint (6 dl) milk
lemon peel
4 oz (100 g) white
  breadcrumbs
1½ oz (40 g) butter

4 oz (100 g) granulated sugar
2 eggs, separated
jam, preferably apricot
2 oz (50 g) caster sugar

Preheat the oven to 350°F/180°C/Regulo 4. Put a strip of lemon
peel into the milk, bring it to simmering point, then pour it on to
the breadcrumbs, stir it well and allow it to cool a little. Heat the
butter until it just melts, then beat it with two ounces (50 g) of the
granulated sugar and the egg yolks. Stir this into the breadcrumbs
and milk mixture, pour it in to a shallow buttered dish and bake
in the oven for three-quarters of an hour, or until the mixture is
fairly well set. Remove it from the oven and spread the top with a
thin layer of jam. Beat the egg whites stiffly, add the remaining
granulated sugar and beat again. Fold in the caster sugar gently
until it is well mixed and then spread this meringue over the jam.
Sprinkle a little more sugar on the meringue, return to the oven
and cook until the top is crisp. Serve hot or cold.

208 Lemon Caramel

Time taken: preparation
15 mins

for the caramel:
4 oz (100 g) sugar
4 tablespoons water

for the custard:
6 oz (175 g) sugar
6 eggs, separated
3½ oz (90 g) butter
1 lemon

Boil together the sugar and water to make the caramel and coat the bottom and sides of a soufflé dish with it. Preheat the oven to 350°F/180°C/Regulo 4. Cream the sugar with the beaten egg yolks, the butter, and the grated peel and the juice of the lemon. Fold in the stiffly beaten egg whites, pour the mixture into the dish and bake in the oven for three-quarters of an hour to an hour. Unmould when cold.

This makes a rather more elaborate version of the crème caramel. It is a rich sweet and should serve at least six people.

209 Lemon Pudding

Time taken: 40 mins

1½ oz (40 g) butter
4 oz (100 g) sugar
4 oz (100 g) flour

4 eggs, separated
1 pint (6 dl) milk
2 lemons

Preheat the oven to 400°F/200°C/Regulo 6. Cream together the butter and sugar. In another bowl mix the flour, the beaten egg yolks, the milk and the juice and grated rind of the two lemons. Add this to the sugar and butter mixture and when well mixed fold in the stiffly beaten egg whites. Pour into a buttered soufflé dish and bake in a *bain-marie* for about half an hour.

This is a simpler lemon dish than the last. It doesn't mind being kept waiting, or being left too long in the oven. It comes out with a spongy top and a custardy base, and can be served hot or cold.

210 Bread and Butter Pudding Time taken: 45 mins

bread slices
3 eggs
2 oz (50 g) vanilla sugar (*or*
   plain sugar and a little
   vanilla essence)

1 pint (6 dl) milk
icing sugar

Preheat the oven to 350°–400°F/180°–200°C/Regulo 5. Line a pie dish with the slices of currant loaf, or white bread, scattered with a few sultanas or raisins. Beat the eggs with the vanilla sugar, and pour the warmed milk over this mixture. Thicken the custard over a gentle heat, then pour it over the bread and bake it in a *bain-marie* for half an hour. The bread will rise to the surface, leaving the custard underneath. Dust the surface with icing sugar and brown under a very hot grill.

You can use a currant loaf for this if you have one, otherwise make it with white bread and scatter some sultanas or raisins on it.

211 Bakewell Tart Time taken: 1 hour

for the pastry:
6 oz (175 g) flour
4 oz (100 g) butter
lemon juice
water

2 eggs and 2 egg yolks
4 oz (100 g) butter
1 tablespoon ground almonds
raspberry jam

Preheat the oven to 400°F/200°C/Regulo 6. Line a flan tin with flaky or shortcrust pastry made from the flour and butter, a little lemon juice and the water. Bake it blind for fifteen minutes.

Reduce the oven temperature to 350°F/180°C/Regulo 4. Beat together the two eggs and the extra yolks, melt the butter, and add it to the eggs with the ground almonds. Spread the pastry base with raspberry jam, pour on the egg mixture and bake in the oven for about half an hour.

212 Snowball Eggs

Time taken: 30–40 mins

4 eggs, separated
4 oz (100 g) vanilla sugar

1 pint (6 dl) milk

Beat the egg whites very stiffly. Mix the vanilla sugar into the milk and bring it to the boil. Poach large tablespoons of the egg white in the milk, turning them over halfway through when they begin to swell. You can make two or three spoonfuls at a time according to the size of the pan. Remove them carefully and put them on to a dish. When all the whites have been poached, beat the yolks and add them to the milk – it prevents curdling if the milk is poured on to the yolks in a bowl and then the whole returned to the saucepan, rather than mixing the yolks straight into the milk. Cook, stirring constantly, until this custard begins to thicken. Remove it and let it cool, and when quite cold pour it round the snowballs in the dish.

213 Meringues

Time taken: preparation 10–15 mins; cooking 40–60 mins

2 egg whites
2 oz (50 g) granulated sugar

2 oz (50 g) caster sugar

Preheat the oven to 250°F/130°C/Regulo ½. Beat the egg whites stiffly, then add the granulated sugar and beat again. Fold in the caster sugar gently until it is well mixed. Line a baking tray with Bakewell parchment (this does not need greasing, and the meringues won't stick) and put spoonfuls of the meringue on to the tray – this amount should make a dozen. Put the tray into the low oven for about half an hour. Then turn the oven off but leave the meringues inside until they are cool. If they are allowed to cool down gradually they are less likely to break than if you subject them to a sudden change of temperature. A teaspoon of coffee or chocolate powder can be added to the mixture if you like. Sandwich them together in pairs with whipped cream, plain or flavoured.

214 Chestnut Meringue

Time taken: 40 mins

for the pastry:
4 oz (100 g) flour
2 oz (50 g) butter
1 teaspoon sugar
1 egg yolk, if available
water

1 tin unsweetened chestnut
purée
1 tablespoon vanilla sugar
for the meringue:
1 egg white
1 oz (25 g) granulated sugar
1 oz (25 g) caster sugar

Preheat the oven to 400°F/200°C/Regulo 6. Make a flan case with the flour, butter and sugar. Bind it with a little water, mixed with the egg yolk if you have one. Bake the flan blind for about fifteen minutes. Reduce the oven temperature to 350°F/180°C/Regulo 4.

When the flan is cool spread the base with the chestnut purée which has been beaten up with the vanilla sugar. Make a meringue (**No 213**) with the egg white and granulated and caster sugar. Spread this over the chestnut and bake in the oven until the meringue is crisp. Leave in the oven to cool a little.

215 Chestnut Cream or Mont Blanc

Time taken: 15–20 mins

1 tin unsweetened chestnut
purée
1 tablespoon vanilla sugar

¼ pint (1.5 dl) double cream
1 egg white

Mix the chestnut purée with the vanilla sugar. Beat up the cream until thick, and fold in the beaten egg white, which makes the cream light. Put the cream in a soft heap on to a serving dish and put the chestnut purée through the coarse sieve of a Mouli or a sieve so that it falls in shreds on to the cream.

Served this way this is sometimes called Chestnut Rice, though there is no rice in it; it can also be served the other way up, with the cream topping the chestnut, in which case it is Mont Blanc.

216 Java Macaroon

Time taken: cooking 1½ hours; finishing 15 mins

4 oz (100 g) ground almonds
8 oz (225 g) sugar
3 egg whites
1½ oz (40 g) butter

for the icing:
4 oz (100 g) icing sugar
1 teaspoon instant coffee
water to mix

toasted almond flakes

Preheat the oven to 350°F/180°C/Regulo 4. Mix the ground almonds and sugar together. Beat two of the egg whites lightly, so that the are frothy but not stiff, and add them to the almonds and sugar. When this is all well mixed, add the other egg white unbeaten, and mix again. Keep back two tablespoons of this mixture as a garnish, put the rest into a prepared tin and bake in the oven for about an hour, or until an inserted skewer comes out clean. Leave it to cool before removing it from the tin. Meanwhile, mix the uncooked mixture with an equal quantity of butter and when the cake is cool spread this over the top. Glaze with the coffee icing and decorate with the toasted almond flakes. Cut it as you would a cake, but it makes a good sweet course.

This is rich and goes a long way. It is also better made at least a day before it is needed. To make it easier to remove it from the tin, either line a tin with Bakewell parchment or foil, or use a tin with a removable base.

217 St Emilion Macaroons

Time taken: 40 mins

4 oz (100 g) ground almonds   3 egg whites
5 oz (150 g) sugar

Preheat the oven to 350°F/180°C/Regulo 4. Mix together the ground almonds and sugar. Beat the egg whites stiffly, then fold them into the almond mixture. Put small spoonfuls on to the prepared baking tray, leaving plenty of space between them as they spread in the cooking. Bake in the oven for about half an hour, or until they are slightly coloured and set.

These small macaroons should also be baked on parchment or foil (*see* **No 213**) so they can be removed from the tray easily.

218 Fruit Meringue

Time taken: 40 mins

2 oz (50 g) dried apricots,
    soaked for about an hour
1 lb (450 g) apples, peeled,
    cored and sliced
1 oz (25 g) sultanas
lemon peel

1 tablespoon sugar, preferably
    brown
butter
for the meringue:
2 egg whites
2 oz (50 g) granulated sugar
2 oz (50 g) caster sugar

Put the soaked apricots in a saucepan with the apples, the sultanas, a strip of lemon peel and the sugar. Add just enough water to prevent the fruit burning, then cook gently until you can mash the fruit to a purée. Add a knob of butter to this.

Preheat the oven to 300°F/150°C/Regulo 2. Beat the egg whites stiffly, add the granulated sugar and beat again, then fold in the caster sugar. Put the fruit into an ovenproof dish, cover with the meringue, sprinkle a very little more sugar on the top (this helps to make the meringue crisp) and bake in the oven for about half an hour. Leave it in the oven after the heat has been turned off if possible, as then the meringue is less likely to crack than if it is brought out straight after cooking.

219 Fruit Crumble

Time taken: preparation
15 mins; cooking 40 mins

1 lb (450 g) fruit, weighed
    after preparation, as
    available
brown sugar

for the top:
4 oz (100 g) flour
4 oz (100 g) sugar
2½ oz (65 g) butter

Preheat the oven to 350°F/180°C/Regulo 4. Put the prepared fruit into a pie dish and sprinkle some brown sugar over it. Mix together the flour, sugar (brown or white) and butter until crumbly, then cover the fruit completely with this mixture. Cook in the oven for about forty minutes until the fruit is cooked and the top golden.

Easier to make than a pie, the crumble mixture seems to be popular with most people. Most fruit can be used, and it is particularly good with apple, rhubarb, gooseberry, blackberry, apricot, or any other fruit that has a marked flavour. The method for making it is the same for all fruit.

220 *Fruit Crunch*

Time taken: preparation 15 mins; cooking 40 mins

This is made the same way as the crumble but the top is made by crushing four ounces of digestive biscuits into crumbs and mixing them with three ounces of melted butter. Bake it as the crumble, or put the mixture over cooked fruit, in which case it will need cooking only for fifteen to twenty minutes.

221 *Creamy Apple Flan*

Time taken: 1 hour

1 lb (450 g) apples
4 oz (100 g) sugar, preferably brown
1 oz (25 g) flour
salt
cinnamon
$\frac{1}{4}$ pint (1.5 dl) cream
1 uncooked pastry case (optional)

Preheat the oven to 375°F/190°C/Regulo 5. Mix together the sugar, flour, and a pinch of salt and of cinnamon. Peel and core the apples and slice them thinly, putting them directly into the flour mixture. Toss the slices in the flour and sugar so that they are well coated, then arrange them on an uncooked pastry case or on a shallow ovenproof dish. Add any of the surplus flour mixture that remains, pour the cream over the apples and bake in a fairly hot oven for about forty minutes or until the apples are cooked. Eat hot, cold or just warm, which is best of all.

This can either be made in a flan case, or if you do not want to use pastry, can be made in an ovenproof dish, which is lighter and easier.

222 *Spicy Apple Turnover*   Time taken: 1 hour

1 lb (450 g) apples, peeled, cored and sliced
1 teaspoon lemon juice
lemon rind
1 teaspoon mixed spice
1 teaspoon sugar
1 oz (25 g) raisins
8 oz (225 g) flaky or shortcrust pastry
1 egg, beaten
caster sugar

Preheat the oven to 450°F/230°C/Regulo 8. Cook the apples gently in just sufficient water to stop them burning. When soft, beat them into a purée and mix in the lemon juice, a little grated lemon rind, and the mixed spice, sugar and raisins.

Roll out the pastry into an oblong and pile the apple mixture up on one half. Brush the edge of the pastry with beaten egg, fold the other half over and press the edges together. Brush the top with beaten egg and sprinkle caster sugar over it. Make one or two diagonal slits in the top of the pastry, put the turnover on to a floured baking tray and cook it in the oven for about twenty-five minutes.

Flaky pastry is best for this, but unless you wish to make it yourself, use flaky pastry mix. This is available everywhere and is excellent.

223 *Tarte Tatin*   Time taken: 40–60 mins

for the pastry:
4 oz (100 g) flour
1 dessertspoon sugar
2 oz (50 g) butter
1 egg
for the caramel:
½ oz (15 g) butter
1 tablespoon water
2 tablespoons sugar

1½ lb (675 g) dessert apples, halved from top to bottom, and cored

Make a shortcrust pastry from the flour, sugar and butter, and bind it with an egg. (You can use flaky pastry if you prefer.) Put it aside to rest.

Meanwhile make a caramel directly on to a seven-inch flan tin. Put the butter, water and sugar into the tin and cook over a moderate heat until the mixture gets well coloured but *don't* let it burn. Preheat the oven to 425°F/220°C/Regulo 7. When the caramel is ready put the apples into the tin, rounded side downwards, to fill the tin as closely as possible. Fill in the gaps with the rest of the apples sliced thinly until the flan is really full, as the apples will shrink in the cooking. Roll the pastry out to a circle large enough to cover the flan tin and bake in the oven for about half an hour. Remove it from the oven, allow it to cool for a few minutes, then reverse the flan on to a serving dish, which brings the apples right side up. The apples should keep their shape but be soft.

224 Baked Apples

Time taken: preparation 10 mins; cooking 30–40 mins

4 large cooking apples
honey
raisins

butter
cream

Preheat the oven to 350°F/180°/Regulo 4. Remove the cores from the apples and score round them horizontally so that the skin is cut, but don't peel them. Put a tablespoon of water into a buttered dish, then put in the apples and fill the centres with a mixture of honey, butter and raisins. Bake in the oven for about half an hour, or until they are cooked and fluffy. Serve them hot with cold whipped cream.

225 Apple Charlotte

Time taken: 30 mins

1 lb (450 g) cooking apples, peeled, cored and sliced
lemon juice
2 tablespoons sugar *or* 1 large tablespoon honey

½ oz (15 g) butter
2–3 slices bread
butter for frying

Add the lemon juice and sugar or honey to the apples, and cook them until the apples are soft enough to make into a purée. Add the butter and leave the purée to cool on the dish in which it is to be served. Cut two or three slices of bread into fingers or squares, heat some butter in a pan and fry the bread bits very crisply. Drain them well and make a roof for the apple purée from them. Sprinkle with sugar and put under a hot grill for the sugar to melt. Serve hot or cold.

226 Fruit Sorbet

Time taken: preparation 20
mins; freezing time 1–2 hours

fruit (see below) to make
½ pint (3 dl) juice

6 oz (175 g) sugar (approx.)
1 pint (6 dl) water

Squeeze the fruit until you have half a pint of juice. Grate a
little of the rind into the juice and let it stand while you dissolve
the sugar in the water by just bringing it to the boil for a few
moments. Let the syrup get cold, then mix it into the juice from
which the rind has been strained. Freeze until set but still rather
mushy. If you have an ice-cream maker, you need do nothing
more about it, but if not it is advisable to turn the refrigerator up
to the highest setting and stir the mixture once or twice.

Use oranges, lemons, grapefruit – whatever you have. A good
proportion is one lemon, one grapefruit and two oranges, but it
can be altered according to what fruit is available. Other fruit
juices, such as blackcurrant or strawberry, can also be used. The
amount of sugar needed will depend on the sweetness of the
fruit, and honey can make a good substitute.

227 Sliced Oranges

Time taken: 15 mins

Cut the rind off three or four oranges, according to size, and peel
them generously so that the white pith is removed as well. Cut
inwards from the outside of the orange, between the membrane
so that the orange segments are loosened and come away without
any skin or pith. If you feel uncertain about doing this, simply
slice the oranges across. Put them into a shallow dish and squeeze
any juice remaining over them. This can also be a very good
dish if a grapefruit is cut in the same way and the fruit slices
alternated in the dish.

This is one of the easiest and most refreshing sweets of all.

228 Caramel Oranges

Time taken: 20–30 mins

Prepare the oranges in the same way as in the recipe above, but
make a syrup from the extra orange juice, two tablespoons of
water and four tablespoons of sugar. Cook until the sugar turns
a golden brown, then pour in a thin layer over the oranges. This

caramel loses its crispness if made too far ahead, so do it at the last possible moment.

229 *Orange Yogurt*　　　　　Time taken: 10 mins

¾ pint (4.5 dl) plain yogurt　　½ lemon
1 large orange　　　　　　　　1 tablespoon sugar

Mix the yogurt with the orange and lemon juice. Add a teaspoon of the grated orange rind and the sugar. Chill well before serving, and if possible make it an hour or so before using, so that the flavour develops. Serve either in one bowl or in individual dishes, and if you like, garnish the top with segments of orange.

This seems to be a favourite with everyone, even those who say they don't like yogurt.

230 *Prune or Apricot Mousse*　　Time taken: 20 mins

1 lb (450 g) dried apricots or　2 eggs, separated
　prunes, soaked for several　　ratafias or macaroons
　hours　　　　　　　　　　　(optional)
1 tablespoon sugar

Cook the fruit in the water in which they soaked until they are soft. Blend into a purée (if using prunes remove the stones) and add sugar to taste. Mix the egg yolks into the fruit purée, beat the egg whites stiffly, fold them into the purée and serve very cold. If using apricots, a few ratafias or macaroons crumbled into the mousse are an improvement.

231 *Sweet Pancakes*　　　Time taken: preparation 10 mins
　　　　　　　　　　　　　　　(in advance); cooking 10 mins

4 oz (100 g) flour　　　　　　½ pint (3 dl) milk and
1 dessertspoon caster sugar　　　water, mixed
1 egg　　　　　　　　　　　　sugar (preferably brown)
　　　　　　　　　　　　　　　lemon

Make the batter: mix the egg and sugar into the flour, then gradually add the liquid, stirring so that the batter is quite smooth,

E

and leave in a cool place for half an hour or more. Stir again before making the pancakes. (See the recipe for savoury pancakes on **No 160**.)

The simplest way of using the pancakes is to roll them up and put them on to a dish as they are made, sprinkle with sugar – brown has more flavour than white – and serve them with lemon.

232 *Cream Cheese Pancakes*   Time taken: 20–30 mins

8 pancakes (**No 231**)
8 oz (225 g) cream cheese (or
  sieved cottage cheese)
1 egg

1 oz (25 g) butter
1 tablespoon vanilla sugar
½ lemon
1 oz (25 g) sultanas

Make eight pancakes as thin as possible and keep them warm between two plates in the oven, unless you are using some that are already made (**No 231**).

For the filling, mix the cream cheese with the egg, butter, vanilla sugar, the grated rind of the half lemon and the sultanas. Fill the pancakes with this mixture, roll them up so that they are fat cylinders and put them side by side on to a shallow dish. Sprinkle the tops with sugar, heat them under a very hot grill so that the sugar browns a little, and serve hot. You can if you like beat up some cream and an egg with the sugar and cover the pancakes with this, which makes the dish very rich and delicious.

233 *Apple Pancakes*   Time taken: 20–30 mins

8 pancakes (above **No 231**)
1 lb (450 g) apples, peeled,
  coved and sliced

1 tablespoon brown sugar
1 oz (25 g) sultanas
lemon rind

Cook the apples with the brown sugar, sultanas, a little lemon rind and just sufficient water to prevent the apples burning. When they are cooked, mash or beat the apples to a purée. Put a line of filling down the centre of each pancake, roll them up, sprinkle with sugar and serve hot.

234 Fritter Batter

3 tablespoons oil
4 oz (100 g) flour
salt

¼ pint (1.5 dl) water
1 egg white

Stir the oil into the flour, add a pinch of salt and the tepid water. Mix until it is a smooth cream and leave it to stand for an hour or so. Just before using, fold in the stiffly beaten egg white.

This differs from the pancake batter in being lighter and crisper.

235 Apple Fritters
Time taken: 20 mins

Make the batter as above (No 234). When ready to use, heat some oil in a pan, dip slices of peeled cored apple into the batter and fry quickly until brown on both sides. Remove and drain well on kitchen paper, and sprinkle with sugar.

Other fruit, such as bananas or pears can be used.

236 Apricot Blancmange
Time taken: 30 mins
plus setting time

½ pint (3 dl) milk
1 oz (25 g) sugar
4 oz (100 g) apricot jam

¼ pint (1.5 dl) double cream
¼ oz (7.5 g) (half a packet) gelatine

Bring the milk to boiling point and add the sugar and jam. Stir until the sugar and jam are dissolved into the milk, then pour this on to the cream and stir until all is mixed and cool. Dissolve the gelatine in a very little water and when dissolved mix it carefully into the blancmange mixture. Pour it into a mould, or small moulds to set.

This dish has become a symbol of bad boarding house or school food, which is a pity as it used to be very good. This is a Victorian recipe and very different from the 'shape' of today. This recipe uses a good apricot jam, but other jams or fruit purées can be used. If the jam is very sweet, cut down on the sugar.

237 St Valentine's Cream   Time taken: 10–15 mins

4 oz (100 g) cream cheese
2 eggs, separated
2 dessertspoons sugar
2 dessertspoons cream

1 teaspoon instant coffee *or* chocolate *or* grated orange rind

Beat together the cream cheese with the egg yolks, sugar and cream. Add the instant coffee (or chocolate or grated orange rind). When the mixture is smooth, fold in the stiffly beaten egg whites. Put the mixture into individual dishes, and keep in the refrigerator until needed, as they are best eaten very cold.

These creams should really be made in heart-shaped moulds, but taste just as good in ordinary ramekins. Use any kind of cream cheese (Philadelphia is good) but not cottage cheese, as its texture is wrong.

238 Tea Cream   Time taken: 20 mins plus setting time

½ oz (15 g) tea
½ pint (3 dl) milk
2 eggs, separated
1 tablespoon sugar

½ oz (1.5 g) (1 packet) gelatine
¼ pint (1.5 dl) double cream

Infuse the tea in the milk by boiling it for a few minutes until the milk becomes coloured. Strain the milk on to the beaten egg yolks which you have mixed with the sugar. Dissolve the powdered gelatine and mix it into the milk mixture. Whip the cream until thick but not stiff and add this. Finally, fold in the stiffly beaten egg whites, pour into a mould which has been rinsed out with cold water, and leave in a cold place to set. Turn it out on to a serving dish when it is set.

If possible use an aromatic China tea for this modern version of an eighteenth-century dish. It can be frozen as ice-cream, in which case leave out the gelatine.

239 Syllabub
Time taken: 15–20 mins

½ lemon
1 tablespoon brandy
1 tablespoon sugar

3 tablespoons medium or
  sweetish sherry
¼ pint (1.5 dl) double cream

Mix the juice and grated rind of the lemon with the brandy, sugar and sherry. Stir until the sugar is dissolved. In another bowl beat up the cream until it starts to thicken, then gradually add the lemon–sherry mixture, beating the cream as you go so that it continues to thicken as it absorbs the liquid. Don't beat so much that it becomes dry. Serve in glasses or ramekins, and chill well. This will keep for a day or so in the refrigerator in a covered bowl.

240 Liqueur Syllabub
Time taken: 10 mins

¼ pint cream
3–4 tablespoons liqueur

sugar, if necessary

If you have any liqueur to hand, this can be made into a syllabub too. Just beat three or four tablespoons into the cream, adding sugar to taste if necessary. Cherry brandy is very good this way, and gives a pretty pink tinge to the cream.

241 Boodle's Fool
Time taken: 20 mins

sponge cake
1 orange
½ lemon

1 dessertspoon sugar
¼ pint (1.5 dl) double cream

Line a dish with pieces of sponge cake cut into slices half an inch (1.25 cm) thick. Grate the rinds of the orange and lemon, and squeeze the juice from the fruit. Mix the rind and juice with the sugar. Beat the cream until it thickens, then add the fruit juice to it, proceeding as for making a syllabub in the preceding recipe. When the cream is thick, pour it over the sponge cakes and chill thoroughly in the refrigerator for at least two hours, longer if possible, so that the juice can penetrate and flavour the cake.

242 *Chocolate Diplomate*   Time taken: 25 mins (in advance); 15 mins to finish

sponge fingers
sponge cake
4 oz (100 g) plain chocolate
2 tablespoons water
1½ oz (40 g) butter
1 egg yolk

for the custard:
½ pint (3 dl) milk
2 tablespoons sugar
1 egg yolk
1 heaped teaspoon cornflour

Butter a cake tin or soufflé dish well. Line the sides with sponge fingers and cover the base of the dish completely with sliced sponge cake cut about half an inch (1.25 cm) thick. Melt the chocolate with the water, then when it is melted add the butter and the beaten egg yolk. Beat until creamy. Pour half of the chocolate mixture over the sponge cake, cover with another layer of cake, then add the remaining chocolate and finish with a third layer of cake. Trim the tops of the sponge fingers so that they are level with the top of the dish, cover with foil, put a weight on top and keep in the refrigerator for an hour or so, or overnight.

Make a thick custard: bring the milk to boiling point with the two tablespoons of sugar. Beat the cornflour into the egg yolk pour the milk on to this, return to the saucepan and stir until the mixture thickens. Leave to cool.

Remove the diplomate from the refrigerator, loosen round the edges and invert it on to a serving dish. If you have some, add a dash of brandy or liqueur to the custard, pour it over the cake, and garnish it, if you like, with grated chocolate.

This is another way of using up sponge cake that may be a bit stale.

243 *Chocolate Mousse*   Time taken: 15 mins

4 oz (100 g) chocolate
1½ oz (40 g) butter

4 eggs, separated

Melt the chocolate over a gentle heat, then add the softened butter and stir until creamy. Mix this with the beaten yolks of the eggs. Beat the egg whites stiffly, then fold them into the chocolate mixture. Put the mixture into individual glasses or ramekins, and keep in the refrigerator until set.

244 Chocolate Almond Pudding

Time taken: preparation
15 mins; cooking 1 hour

3 eggs, separated
2 oz (50 g) plain chocolate,
   grated
2 oz (50 g) butter
2 oz (50 g) ground almonds
2 oz (50 g) sugar

for the sauce:
1½ oz (40 g) chocolate
2 tablespoons milk
¼ oz (7.5 g) butter

whipped cream

Butter and flour a pudding basin. Cream the yolks of the eggs and the chocolate, butter, ground almonds and sugar. Beat the egg whites stiffly and fold them into the chocolate cream. Pour into the prepared basin, leaving about an inch at the top for the pudding to swell, cover the top with foil and steam for an hour. Turn out of the basin as soon as possible and serve hot or cold with whipped cream and a chocolate sauce made by melting together the chocolate, butter and milk.

245 Apricot Poached Eggs

Time taken: 20 mins

4 slices bread
butter *or* oil for frying
2–3 tablespoons double cream

4 apricot halves, fresh,
   tinned *or* dried and
   reconstituted

Cut out with a pastry cutter a round from each slice of bread. Fry the rounds crisply in butter or oil, drain and cool. Whip up the cream until thick, then spread it on the fried bread, or pipe it round the edges. Press an apricot half on to the middle of each, cut side downwards, so that they resemble poached eggs.

246 Ice-Cream

Time taken: preparation
20 mins plus freezing time

¾ pint (4.5 dl) milk
2 whole eggs, and 2 yolks

2 oz (50 g) vanilla sugar
½ pint (3 dl) double cream

Heat the milk and pour it on to the eggs and extra yolks and sugar. Return the mixture to the saucepan and thicken it like a custard. Leave it to cool, then mix in the cream, whipped until it is thick but not dry. Mix well and put into the freezer tray of the refrigerator, which should be turned up to its highest setting. It is advisable to stir it once or twice while it is freezing to prevent crystals forming. If you have an ice-cream maker, there is no need to alter the refrigerator setting or to stir.

This is the basic custard, but it can be flavoured at will, with chocolate, coffee or blackcurrant syrup or served with chopped angelica, cherries and sultanas mixed in.

247 *Pink Panther Pudding*   Time taken: 10 mins

Mix a tablespoon or more or less of blackcurrant syrup into a carton of plain yogurt, chill and serve. Some sweet-toothed people might like some sugar added, but this is a matter of taste.

Simplest of all, and much liked by children – and grown-ups. It is one of the puddings that have no real recipe – they just happen.

248 *Cream Cheese and Apricots*   Time taken: 10 mins

The sticky preserved apricots that can be bought in health shops keep well and make an easy and delicious fruit course; serve them with cream cheese. Nothing more, nothing less. Put a mound of cream cheese (Philadelphia is good) on to a dish and surround it with the apricots.

249 *Home-Made Yogurt*   Time taken: overnight

Stir a tablespoon of instant milk powder into a pint of milk. Bring it just to the boil, then let it cool to about 100°F 230°C. If you haven't a thermometer around, this is when the milk feels comfortably warm to the touch.

Stir in a large teaspoon of plain yogurt, mix well and pour it either into a wide-necked vacuum flask, or into small pots with lids. If you use a vacuum flask, cork it up and leave it alone (easier to do at this stage, but more difficult to get out afterwards). If you are using small pots, put them into an insulated bag, with a hot sachet underneath, and any gaps between them filled in with newspaper. Or pour the yogurt into your chosen container and put it in the airing cupboard for several hours. The object of all this is to keep the milk warm for long enough to let the yogurt 'take'. The next day the yogurt should be set rather like junket. Keep a spoonful of this mixture back as your starter for the next batch. This home-made kind is never quite as firm as the commercial ones, but very good, much cheaper than buying it, and always available, even when the shops have shut.

Odds and ends

THIS SECTION INCLUDES various suggestions for keeping the wolf from the door at different times of day. There are recipes for quickly made bread and biscuits for tea, or for filling up ravenous children or guests back from an energetic walk. There are also ideas for nibbles to go with drinks when your guests show no sign of leaving, or you know that dinner won't be ready for an hour, or you are having to stretch a meal to accommodate them and want to fill them up a bit first.

Some of these titbits you can keep in the store-cupboard: bacon rinds, fried very slowly and gently until the fat runs from them and they become dry and crisp, are delicious. So are small pieces of chicken skin, sprinkled with salt and cooked in exactly the same way. These are known as Gribenies and are a Jewish delicacy. Keep them in an airtight container and use the chicken fat for cooking vegetables or making pastry.

Croustades of fried bread make the basis of useful snacks and keep their crispness well. Cut slices of bread a good inch thick, remove the crusts, and cut them into rounds with a pastry cutter. Using a smaller cutter score the middle of each round about two thirds deep and scoop out the middle. Deep fry these bread cases in hot oil, drain well, and when cold fill them like vol-au-vent cases.

You can also make the herb cheese (**No 255**) and cream cheese dip (**No 254**) and eke them out with plain biscuits or crisps or rounds of bread cut out with a pastry cutter, and baked in the oven until dry.

250 Soda Bread

Time taken: 1 hour

1 lb (450 g) flour, brown,
white or a mixture of each
1 teaspoon salt
1 teaspoon bicarbonate of soda

½–¾ pint (3–4 dl) sour milk
(or fresh milk with a
spoonful of vinegar or
half milk, half yogurt)

Preheat the oven to 400°F/200°C/Regulo 6. Mix the flour with the salt and bicarbonate of soda. Add about half a pint of sour milk and with a wooden spoon mix to a dough which should be moist but not sloppy. You may need a little more liquid, as flour varies in its consistency. Grease a loaf tin well and put the dough into this, making a shallow indentation down the middle so that the bread will rise evenly. Bake in the oven for about forty-five minutes or until the loaf sounds hollow when you knock on the base of the tin. Turn it out as soon as possible to cool on a wire rack, and leave it until it is quite cold before cutting. If you have no loaf tin, this can be put in a heap on a baking tray and cooked as it is.

This is very quickly made as it needs no rising time. It is best made with wholemeal flour, but any flour will do. Anyone interested in breadmaking with yeast would do well to get hold of a copy of *The Baking of an English Loaf* written by Elizabeth David with her usual skill, but, alas, now out of print.

251 Spice Bread

Time taken: preparation
10–15 mins; cooking 1½ hours

10 oz (285 g) self-raising flour
½ teaspoon mixed spice
1 teaspoon ginger
6 oz (175 g) sultanas
4 oz (100 g) brown sugar

2 oz (50 g) butter
6 oz (175 g) syrup or honey
1 egg
6 tablespoons milk

Preheat the oven to 350°F/180°C/Regulo 4. Mix flour with the mixed spice and ginger, then add the sultanas and brown sugar. Melt the butter with the syrup or honey and stir this into the flour, together with the egg beaten up in the milk. Mix well together, pour into a well-greased loaf tin and bake for an hour and a half in the oven. Turn out as soon as possible and cool on a wire rack; if possible leave the loaf for a day before cutting.

This is halfway between bread and cake, and useful as either at teatime.

252 Sweet Biscuits   Time taken: 20 mins

1 egg   2 oz (50 g) butter, melted
2 oz (50 g) vanilla sugar   2 oz (50 g) self-raising flour

Preheat the oven to 450°F/230°C/Regulo 7, and butter two baking trays. Beat the egg with the vanilla sugar until thick, then add the melted butter and the flour. Mix together well, then put small teaspoonfuls of the mixture on to one of the baking sheets leaving plenty of space between them as they spread in the cooking. Bake for about ten minutes or until the biscuits are coloured and the edges turning brown. Take them off the tray as soon as possible and cool on a wire rack. They get brittle when they are cooling, so do this quickly. It is easier to do one tray at a time, baking the second lot as you remove the first ones from the tray

These are good for serving with creamy desserts or fruit fools. The flavour can be altered by using a few drops of almond essence or orange-flower water.

253 Cheesy Biscuits   Time taken: 25 mins

4 oz (100 g) self-raising flour   4 oz (100 g) butter
1 oz (25 g) cheese, grated   ½ teaspoon salt

Preheat the oven to 350°F/180°C/Regulo 4, and grease a flat baking tray. Mix the flour with the grated cheese, the butter, which should be soft but not melted, and the salt. Knead quickly until it becomes a workable dough, then either pipe small biscuits on the baking tray or roll into small marble-sized balls. Put them on to the tray and bake for about fifteen minutes, until they are just coloured.

These are good to serve with drinks, and quickly made.

254 Cream Cheese Dip

Time taken: 10 mins

8 oz (225 g) Philadelphia cream cheese

4 oz (100 g) plain yogurt

1 tablespoon (or more) tomato purée

1 heaped teaspoon curry powder

1 tooth garlic, crushed

1 teaspoon paprika

1 teaspoon Angostura bitters

1 tablespoon, chopped parsley

Mix together until smooth the Philadelphia cheese and yogurt. Add the tomato purée, curry powder, garlic, paprika, Angostura, a little salt and the parsley. Mix so that all the ingredients blend together and leave for an hour or so if possible so that the flavours can mix. The ingredients can be adjusted in quantity at will.

Serve with biscuits to dip in, or with chopped-up raw vegetables, such as carrots, celery or cauliflower sprigs.

This dip can be used as a snack with drinks, or as a first course.

255 Herb Cheese

Mix four ounces (100 g) of soft cream cheese, or a mixture of cream and cottage cheese (but sieve the cottage cheese first) with a selection of chopped fresh herbs such as parsley, mint and chives particularly, and others to taste. Add a little salt, and use sufficient herbs to make the cheese look well speckled with green. Serve with plain biscuits.

This calls for fresh herbs, so if you haven't any, forget this recipe and try the next one.

256 Liptauer

Mix the cream and cottage cheese as above, then work into it a big teaspoon of paprika – enough to give the cheese a good pink tinge – a teaspoon of chopped capers, a chopped gherkin and a teaspoon of caraway seeds with a little salt. If the cheese is rather dry, mix in a little softened butter.

This is more of a winter version of the herb cheese.

Index

As well as the names of individual dishes this index includes bold headings for the main ingredients used by the resourceful cook – cheese, eggs, potatoes, tomatoes, the various tinned or preserved staples, and so on – showing the dishes which can be made partly or mainly from them. We have assumed that *small* quantities of such staples as seasonings and herbs, milk, butter, oil for frying, sugar, onions, flour and single eggs, will usually be available, and have only indexed these ingredients when they are the main, or an essential, ingredient in a large quantity. Also, if you have *no* stock of one staple ingredient you will find dishes which do *not* require it indexed as

Milk, main dishes not requiring
    puddings not requiring

and so on. Numbers in bold refer to recipes. Other references are to page numbers.